street-chic jewellery

Susie Johns

street-chic jewellery

NEW
HOLLAND

First published in 2009
by New Holland Publishers (UK) Ltd
London • Cape Town • Sydney • Auckland

Garfield House
86–88 Edgware Road
London W2 2EA
United Kingdom
www.newhollandpublishers.com

80 McKenzie Street
Cape Town 8001
South Africa

Unit 1, 66 Gibbes Street
Chatswood
NSW 2067
Australia

218 Lake Road
Northcote
Auckland
New Zealand

ISBN 978 1 84773 171 5

Senior Editor: Corinne Masciocchi
Designer: Lucy Parissi
Photographer: Paul Bricknell
Production: Marion Storz
Editorial Direction: Rosemary Wilkinson

2 4 6 8 10 9 7 5 3 1

Reproduction by Pica Digital Pte Ltd, Singapore
Printed and bound by Craft Print International Ltd, Singapore

contents

introduction

Custom-made jewellery is not only fun to wear – and a great way to express your individuality and sense of style – it is great fun to make.

The simplest necklace is made by stringing beads on to a length of thread and knotting the two ends together – what could be easier? But you may wish to be a bit more ambitious. What about shorter necklaces? Or multi-strand necklaces? How do you add a fastening? How do you keep the strands separate or finish off the ends? How can you attach charms?

Of course, as well as necklaces there are bracelets, earrings and brooches, too – all of which you will find, in various guises, in the pages of this book.

This book does not aim to be a comprehensive guide to jewellery-making but it does tackle some of the basic techniques and offers plenty of tips to help give your hand-made creations a professional-looking finish. The projects are very varied

Pin-ups

These portrait pins are a great way to put someone in the frame, be it rock star, actor or historical hero. Turn to pages 68–9 to find out how to make them.

and have been created using not only beads and chains but some more unusual materials in order to offer a wide range of styles to suit most tastes. There are beaded necklaces, bracelets and earrings – some more conventional than others – and there are badges and wrist cuffs, rag corsages and charm pins. Many of the projects use beads

Waterfall

Lightweight plastic beads are an ideal choice for dangly earrings. Experiment with different beads: long, thin shapes such as these blue beads seem to work best. You'll find full instructions on pages 96–7.

6

Just for fun
On pages 100–01, find out how to make dramatic hoop earrings, then have fun with different coloured beads and various dangles and charms. Here, small plastic dalmatians are hung using screw eyes, and black, white and red beads have been used to follow the colour scheme.

8

and some use fabrics, cords, lace, paint or paper, too. The other good thing is that, as well as shiny new components from your local craft shop or bead emporium, you can, if you wish, incorporate broken jewellery, found objects and bits of old junk, which should particularly appeal to anyone with a conscience. We are in the midst of a revival right now, where it is cool to recycle and even more cool to be creative.

So let's get started. As well as more than 30 individual projects, all of them with clear step-by-step instructions and many of them with suggested variations on the main theme, there is a gallery section at the back of the book: be inspired by eight pages of additional pieces, all created using similar techniques to those used throughout the book and displayed here to help get your creative juices flowing. Once you have mastered the basic techniques – whether it's rolling paper beads, converting buttons into charms, or transferring pictures on to fabric – you can come up with your own ideas and create your own unique pieces.

If a particular project appeals to you, all the information is there on the page to allow you to make your own exact replica. But you should also be able to add your own special touch, if you want to. You could, for instance, make a necklace shorter or longer; add a few extra dangles to a brooch or

Cute as a button
Here's a quick and easy idea using two-hole buttons: simply thread them on to beading elastic, bringing the elastic up from the back through one of the holes, back down through the other hole, then through the next button in the same way. This creates a double layer of buttons, sitting back-to-back. For the average wrist you will need 20 buttons, 16–18 mm (⅝ in) in diameter. For more ideas using buttons, check out pages 76–7.

earrings; paint a papier mâché badge in your own colour scheme; and stitch some sequins on to your fabric cuff.

Look at the examples on these pages: they are all extensions of the main projects and are shown here to provide you with even more inspiration. They also combine to show you that jewellery-making can cater for all tastes, from the exotic to the bizarre and from the homely to the hilarious.

Are you a punk or a princess? A hippy or a diva? Rock chick or raver? Modernist or retro queen? Flick through the pages of this book and you are sure to find something to express your style. Making your own jewellery can make you stand out from the crowd, invite admiring glances and even requests to make stuff for your family, friends or even complete strangers. What are you waiting for?

Stitched

With fabric and thread, you can convey a subtle slogan. You could even make a name badge, or send a special message to someone. The choice is yours. To find out how to express yourself with thread, turn to pages 72–3.

Patch test

Patches are fun to make and are so versatile: you can pin them onto coats, jackets, shirts and even pockets! Turn to pages 70–1 to find out more.

9

All squared up

These square plastic discs make a bright retro-style bracelet. They are simply attached to a length of cable chain with jump rings. Turn to pages 76–77 to find out how.

materials

When it comes to collecting the basic materials and equipment, making your own jewellery can seem complex and maybe a little confusing for the novice.

Beads

The shapes and sizes available are overwhelming – not to mention the colours. Beads are made from all kinds of materials, including plastic, glass, stone, wood and metal, and in many different shapes: round, faceted, square, saucer-shaped, discs, tubes and barrels, to name but a few. If you cannot find the exact match for any of the beads used in this book, you should be able to choose a suitable substitute.

When selecting beads, it is easy be distracted by their beauty but there are some practical considerations to be made, too. For instance, if you are intending to make a long necklace, you may not want to choose very heavy beads; the same applies to dangly earrings which may drag on your earlobes unless you use lightweight components. Long beads may not work well on a short necklace and very small beads, which can be fiddly and time-consuming to thread, may try your patience when making a longer necklace, so you may prefer to choose something chunkier and quicker to complete. And if the beads you set your heart on cost a lot to buy, you may want to buy some less expensive ones to go in between.

Small glass beads are plentiful and versatile. The round ones, rocailles, are graded by size, with the smallest ones sometimes being referred to as seed beads. In this book, sizes 6/0, 7/0 and 9/0 have been used most frequently and the size required for a project will be specified in the list of materials.

Rocailles are the beads traditionally used for embroidery and woven techniques. They are also invaluable for use as spacer beads between larger or fancier beads, or as stoppers to prevent beads with larger holes falling off the end of a strand of thread or a pin.

Small glass beads – including the tube-shaped bugle beads – are available in dozens of colours and can be opaque, transparent, iridescent, metallic, pearlised or with silver linings that reflect the light beautifully. They are usually sold by weight or volume, or in strings, and this is an economical way to buy them. If you need only a few, however, then many outlets sell them in small packs or clear acrylic tubes.

10

Larger glass beads, plain or fancy, can be purchased singly for a pendant, in pairs for earrings, or in larger quantities to make a special bracelet or necklace.

Metal beads can create a luxurious effect used alone or in conjunction with other components. One of the disadvantages of metal, whether brass, copper or silver, old or new, is that it tends to discolour over time. Metallic beads made from glass, plastic or other materials can create a similar effect at a fraction of the cost.

Plastic is a great material for fun, frivolous jewellery. Look for novelty plastic beads in toy shops as well as bead suppliers, and search out vintage bead treasures in the form of broken necklaces, brooches and bracelets in thrift stores and markets – or raid your grandmother's bead box.

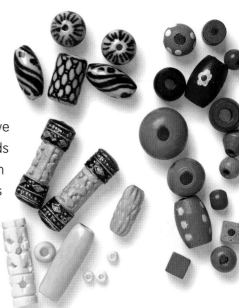

Other materials include wood, bone, shell and clay, all of which produce distinctive beads useful for all kinds of purposes. The brooch on pages 64–5 features small clay beads while the necklaces on pages 46–7 employ wooden beads.

Buttons can be incorporated into jewellery in a number of ways and lend a particular character and quirkiness. Like beads, they come in different shapes, sizes and materials and can be bought new or second-hand.

Charms are items that can be hung from chains, earrings, pins and other components. They may already have some kind of hole or ring. You can create a charm by adding a ring or loop to, say, a small plastic or wooden toy, to allow it to be attached to a necklace or bracelet. Buy charms from the same places you buy beads and other supplies, or search online for vintage or more unusual items by typing in the keywords 'charms', 'crackerjack prizes' or 'gumball charms'.

Findings

Jump rings come in a number of sizes and finishes and are used for joining various components together or for attaching charms to chains or other threading material. The sizes used throughout this book are 3 mm, 5 mm and 8 mm. If no specific size is stated in a project, choose the smallest size that is practical to use.

Screw eyes and pendant beads. Screw eyes from DIY stores can be used to convert a small wooden or plastic item into a charm. Look out also for pendant beads, with a loop for hanging a charm, which are useful for making items such as the chokers on pages 40–1.

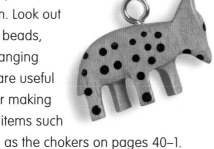

Headpins and **eyepins** are used to make dangles. Choose an eyepin if you wish to add a charm to the end, or a headpin if you want a plain end. Remember that if the bead you are threading on to the headpin has a large hole, first thread on a smaller bead to hold the larger bead in place.

12

Crimps are a group of findings used mostly for finishing the ends of threads and cords – though some have other uses too.

• **Flat end crimps**, or **box crimps**, are used to form links on the ends of leather thongs, flat cords or narrow ribbons.

• **Calotte crimps**, shaped like a clam shell, are useful for creating a neat finish by hiding knots and loose ends. They have a small loop to which a fastening or jump ring can be attached.

• **Cord end crimps** are good for round cords and thongs, or multiple strands of finer cords.

• **Lace end crimps** are available in a number of widths and are ideal for finishing the ends of ribbons and braids or wider strips of leather, and joining them with jump rings to other components (see pages 42–3).

• **Crimp beads** are tiny beads made from soft metal that can be used instead of knots to hold beads in place. The round, fluted ones are sometimes called French crimps. You can buy special crimping pliers for squashing crimp beads but flat-nose pliers will do the job just as well.

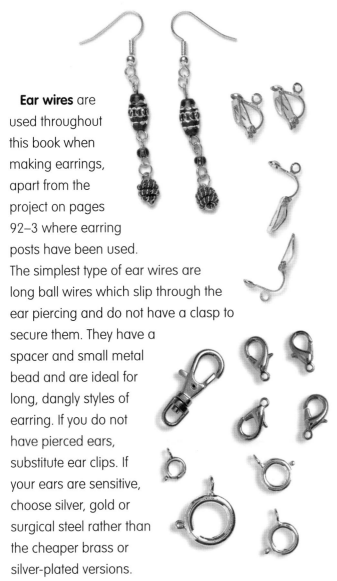

Ear wires are used throughout this book when making earrings, apart from the project on pages 92–3 where earring posts have been used. The simplest type of ear wires are long ball wires which slip through the ear piercing and do not have a clasp to secure them. They have a spacer and small metal bead and are ideal for long, dangly styles of earring. If you do not have pierced ears, substitute ear clips. If your ears are sensitive, choose silver, gold or surgical steel rather than the cheaper brass or silver-plated versions.

Closures, such as lobster claw clasps, also known as carab clasps, and bolt rings have been used throughout the book, though other types of fastenings are available. For heavy necklaces, you may want to use the type of clasp, similar to a lobster claw often used for key rings or attaching handbag straps.

Pins, including safety pins, brooch backs, hatpins and kilt pins, all have uses in hand-

crafted jewellery, so make sure you have a good supply. Look out for special 'charm' pins, too, which have integral loops for attaching charms.

Perforated discs provide a firm base for intricate beadwork and are available in a few different sizes, making them suitable for earrings as well as brooches and pendants. Rings sometimes include a perforated disc, a flat disc on to which you can glue a jewel or other flat-backed component, or metal loops for attaching beads and charms.

13

Spacer bars are used to separate strands of beads when making multi-stranded bracelets (such as the one on pages 78–9) and necklaces. There are several different sizes and styles available, usually with between three and six holes, and they are generally used with end bars to which a fastening can be attached.

Fabrics and threading materials

Fabrics for jewellery-making, because of the small scale, are rarely more than scraps so it is not necessary to go out and buy something specially. For the few projects in this book that use fabric, simply raid your sewing basket – or someone else's – for a few choice pieces.

Ribbons and braids also come into their own for making chokers or adding details to various projects, such as the patches on pages 70–1 and the fabric medal on pages 72–3.

Chains are easy to work with and give hand-made pieces a very professional finish. Use measured lengths for necklaces and bracelets and save small pieces for making links and fastenings, extending necklaces and chokers, attaching charms or adding a decorative element to all kinds of projects.

14 Adhesives

Instant bond glue can be applied to knots – just a tiny drop will suffice – for extra security. Choose a tube with a hollow wire nozzle to allow easy application on a small scale.

Metal glue or any all-purpose glue recommended for joining at least one metal surface is a good choice for attaching faux jewels and securing findings such as eyepins and screw eyes to paper, plastic or other materials. Epoxy resin, a two-part glue, is one of the best choices but some people find it more fiddly and time-consuming than some of the instant bond glues that are available.

Découpage medium is used for projects involving paper, to create rolled paper beads, bases for brooches and earrings, or to apply paper cutouts. A final coat or two brushed over the surface seals and protects, giving a glossy finish.

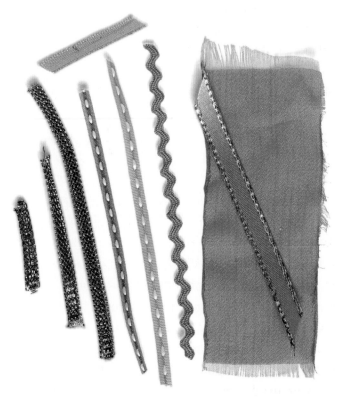

Transfer papers, available from most stationery suppliers, are great for transferring images. Be sure to choose a type suitable for your printer or photocopier: either inkjet or laser. Fabrics recommended for applying transfers are usually white and with a high cotton content; they should also be pre-washed and ironed.

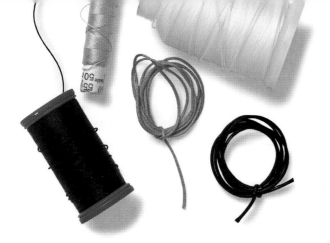

Silk beading thread or specialist threads made from nylon or nylon-coated wire are all useful for stringing small beads – but fishing line or dental floss are good substitutes. For stitching beads to fabric, a strong sewing thread can be used.

Cords made from synthetic threads, linen or waxed cotton, and leather thongs, either flat or round, are also useful depending on the size of beads or charms and the look you are trying to achieve.

Elastic, the kind specially designed for beading, is useful for making bracelets with tiny components. For larger beads, any strong cord elastic will do.

Wire is invaluable for making fastenings such as those used to create the charm bracelet on pages 76–7 from buttons. The wire used in most of the projects in this book is 0.6 mm silver-plated brass wire; this is a medium thickness, strong enough to support medium-weight beads and charms, reasonably easy to bend yet soft enough to cut with an old pair of scissors if you do not have wire cutters in your tool box. Look out also for coloured wires.

Other materials

Leather has been used in one or two of the projects, either as a featured material or to glue to the back of a piece to give a neat finish. It can also be cut, using a craft knife and metal ruler, into thin strips or thongs, which have a number of uses in jewellery-making. Small leather scraps are relatively inexpensive to buy.

Shrink plastic (see pages 50–1) comes in flat sheets ready to decorate with felt tips, pencils or rubber stamps. When decorated, cut out the shape and place it in a domestic oven to shrink. Alternatively you could use a heat tool. Be sure to read the manufacturer's instructions carefully before you embark on a project that uses shrink plastic.

tools

Unless you are going to take up jewellery-making as a serious hobby or profession, you will not wish to outlay too much money on tools, so you will be pleased to know that not many specialist tools are required and that it may be possible to utilise ones you probably already have in the house or workshop.

Round-nose pliers (1) are used to bend wire into a neat loop or 'eye'.

Flat-nose pliers (2) are useful for opening jump rings, holding small components and flattening crimps. Sometimes you may find it necessary to use two pairs of pliers, one in each hand, but will more than likely be able to manage with one.

Wire cutters (3) are useful but not essential: all the wire used in this book is of a very fine gauge (no thicker than 0.6 mm) and can be easily cut with an old pair of scissors.

Crimping pliers (4) are useful for squashing crimp beads but if you don't have a pair don't worry – flat-nose pliers as just as good.

Bead reamers (5) are used to enlarge holes in some beads or to smooth rough surfaces. They are not a vital piece of equipment for the beginner but something you might wish to consider adding to your kit if you become an enthusiastic beader.

Scissors (6) are always useful: small, pointed ones for cutting intricate shapes from paper, embroidery scissors for cutting thread, and dressmaking scissors for fabrics – though a good all-purpose pair will probably suffice for all these jobs.

Ballpoint pens or **pencils (7)** will be needed for marking fabric, leather, paper and other materials. When marking fabric, it is best to use a pencil as the lines can be erased more easily.

Plastic and metal rulers (8) will come in useful for measuring threads, ribbons and strings of beads, as well as marking straight lines on fabric, paper or leather.

A **craft knife (9)** is more useful than scissors in some instances, and for cutting straight lines you will also need a metal straight edge and a cutting mat.

Beading needles (10) are long and with a very narrow eye that will pass through the tiniest of holes when stringing beads or stitching them to fabric. Short, sharp sewing needles can also be useful, and even darning needles for thicker threads or cords and beads with larger apertures.

Crochet hooks (11) sizes 1.75 mm and 3mm are used for two of the projects in this book.

A **spring punch (12)** serves the same purpose as a leather punch. Both tools come in handy when punching holes in leather. If you enjoy scrapbooking or card-making, you may already have one in your tool kit.

techniques

There are no special skills to master before you embark on the projects in this book. Once you have all the materials and tools you need, the instructions that accompany each project will help you on your way to achieving fabulous results. The following techniques will, however, help novice beaders to understand some basic methods, especially when using components you may not have encountered before. And, of

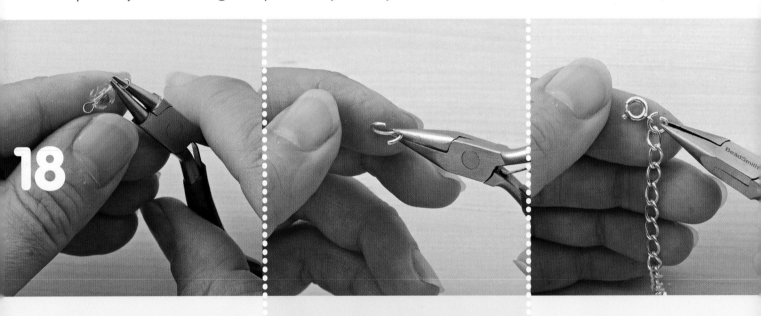

To form a loop on the end of a piece of wire or a headpin, use round-nose pliers. The pliers have two cone-shaped pincers and this allows you to make a smaller or larger ring shape depending on what position along the cone you grip the wire. Make sure not to leave a gap in the loop. For added security, you may wish to overlap the end of the wire to ensure that the loop is completely closed.

The correct way to open and close a jump ring is to use a sideways 'scissor' action – don't pull them open. You can hold the ring between your fingers or, if you find this difficult, try using a second pair of flat-nose pliers. When closing the ring, bring the ends back together – there should be no gap between the ends.

To attach a clasp to the end of a necklace or bracelet, use a jump ring. Open the ring, slip on the two elements to be joined, and close the ring securely.

course, each project is explained using illustrated step-by-step instructions so you should have no trouble in making your own wearable works of art. Remember: if you are making a long necklace that will pass over your head without the need for any kind of fastening, the only technique you need is tying a firm knot. But if your necklace or bracelet requires a fastening, check out the tips on using jump rings and crimps.

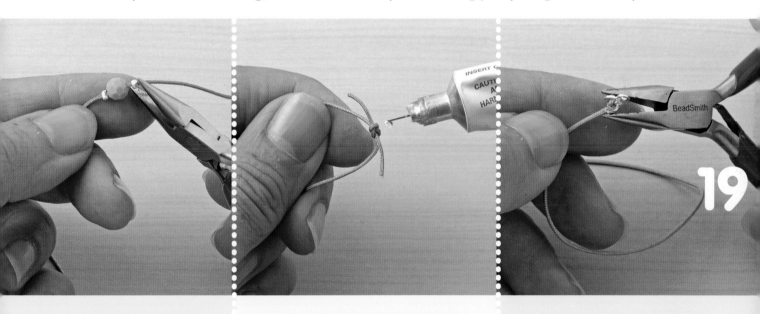

Crimp beads are used to secure thread ends. Thread the crimp on to the thread, then pass the thread through the clasp or other finding you wish to attach. Pass the short end of the thread back through the crimp bead. Using flat-nose pliers (or crimping pliers if you have them), crush the crimp. Gently tug the thread end to make sure you have squashed the crimp well enough to hold the thread in place; if not, squeeze it again with the pliers.

When knotting thread ends on a necklace, it is a good idea to seal the knot to prevent it from coming undone. To do this, apply a very small blob of quick-drying all-purpose glue. Jewellery suppliers sell suitable glues in tubes with a fine wire applicator for accurate application – but you could use a pin, short length of wire or the end of a toothpick to apply the glue to the right spot.

A calotte crimp is a neat way to finish the ends of a necklace when you wish to attach a clasp or other fastening. Knot the thread and apply a blob of glue, then place the thread end across the calotte with the knot lying inside the clamshell shape: the short end near the loop and the long end through the small indentation. Squeeze shut then trim off the short end of the thread. Calotte crimps can also be used to cover a flattened crimp bead.

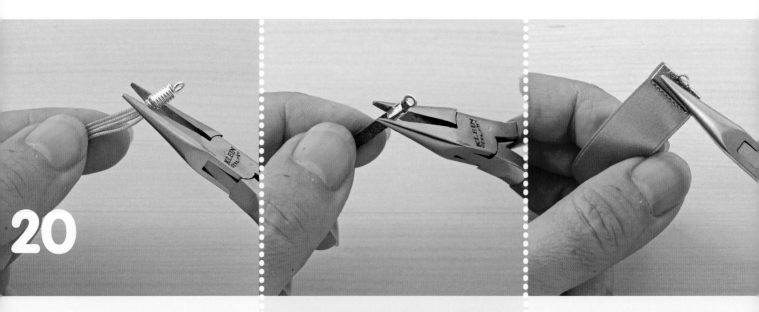

20

A cord end crimp is used on the ends of round cords. Slip the ends of the cord into the coil and squeeze the last ring of the coil so that it flattens against the cord. If the cord end has a tendency to fray, bind it with thread before inserting into the coil (see pages 36–7).

Box crimps are generally used to attach clasps to the ends of flat-cut leather thongs. Use flat-nose pliers to squash the flat sides of the crimp on to the leather.

Lace end crimps, available in different sizes to fit different widths of ribbon, braid or flat strips of leather, are useful when you want to neaten the end and attach a link or clasp. Simply insert the end of the material you are using, then use flat-nose pliers to squeeze the two sides of the crimp together.

Some threads are stiff enough to pass through beads without using a needle. A beading needle is useful, however, for soft threads and small beads, and essential for stitching beads on to fabric.

A leather punch is the best tool for making neat holes in leather. You may not want to invest in this specialist tool unless you are intending to do a lot of leatherwork – though it comes in handy as a household tool for adding extra holes to leather belts.

For punching holes in leather, you could also try using a spring punch. This is a tool used by scrapbookers and card-makers and if you enjoy these hobbies you may already have one in your tool kit. Place the leather on a cutting mat, place the punch in position where you wish the hole to be, then lift the top of the punch and allow it to spring back, punching a neat hole.

necklaces

tools and materials

Old magazines or brochures
Ruler
Pencil
Scissors or craft knife
Crochet needle or skewer
Glue stick
Découpage medium
Paintbrush
Silver seed beads
11 silver headpins
22 disc-shaped ivory-coloured beads
Round-nose pliers
Silver jump rings
40 cm (16 in) silver chain link
10 silver charms
Silver lobster claw clasp

sunday supplement

They may not survive a rainstorm but on a sunny summer's day these colourful beads will brighten up any outfit. Have fun selecting magazine pages with large areas of colour and experiment with paper strips of different widths to make a colourful assortment of beads. This is a fun activity that children can participate in – but though these beads are child's play to make, the finished results can be quite sophisticated, as the charm necklace, with its pretty pastel colours and shimmer of silver, goes to prove.

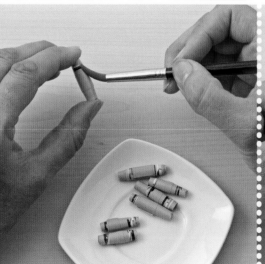

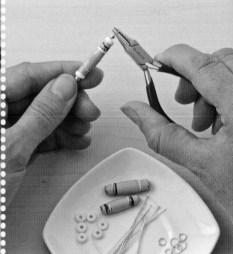

1 Cut long strips, between 2 and 4 cm (¾ and 1½ in) at one end, tapering to between 2 and 5 mm (1/12 and ¼ in) at the other end. Starting at the wider end, roll the strip around a crochet hook or skewer. After the halfway point, apply glue to the back of the strip and continue rolling.

2 Give the finished bead a coat or two of découpage medium and leave to dry.

3 Thread a small silver seed bead on to a headpin, followed by an ivory disc bead, then the paper bead, another ivory disc bead and another silver bead. Using the round-nose pliers, bend the end of the wire to form a closed loop.

Roll-up

For a simple necklace, cut a length of cord or string about 5 cm (2 in) longer than you want the finished necklace to be. Sort the beads into batches of the same, or similar, colours, then thread paper beads and plastic beads alternately on to the cord. If the necklace is long enough to slip over your head, simply knot the ends of the cord together. For a shorter necklace, you will need to add a fastening.

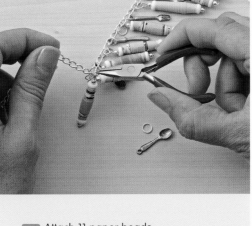

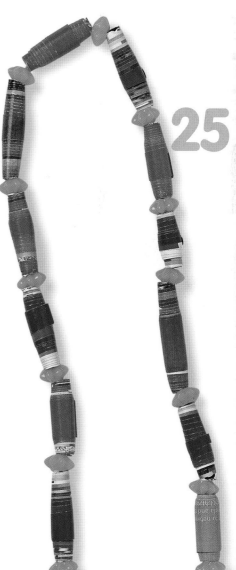

25

4 Slip a jump ring through the loop you have created and use it to attach the bead to the centre link in the chain.

5 Attach 11 paper beads, alternating with silver charms. Leave one chain link free between each charm and bead. Attach the lobster claw clasp to one end of the chain using a 5 mm (¼ in) jump ring, and attach an 8 mm (⁵⁄₁₆ in) jump ring to the other.

tools and materials

Printed paper (telephone directory or old dictionary)
Ruler
Scissors or craft knife
18 silver or pearl disc beads
18 silver headpins
Découpage medium
Paintbrush
18 silver barrel beads
Round-nose pliers
17 safety pins
Green, blue and turquoise rocailles
50 cm (20 in) silver link chain
36 x 5 mm silver jump rings
Silver lobster claw clasp
8 mm silver jump ring

hidden message

Though this necklace looks sophisticated, it is created from humble safety pins and scraps of paper. Look carefully and you can read the words on the printed paper used to create these hand-made beads. If you want to keep your message secret, use a language that is not your own – such as Welsh or Greek, perhaps?

Try making one paper bead before cutting all 18 strips required, as you may need to make the strips slightly longer or shorter, depending on the diameter of the holes in the barrel beads and how tightly you roll the paper.

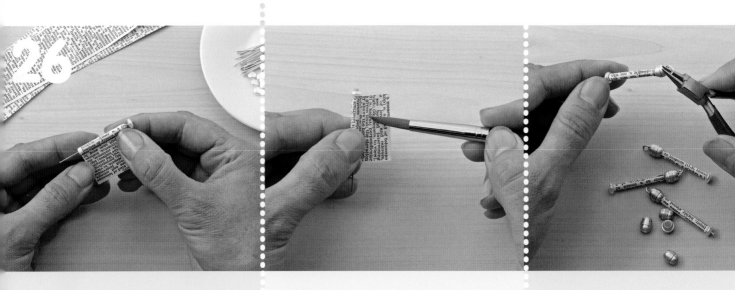

1 Cut a strip of paper measuring approximately 18 x 3 cm (7 x 1¼ in) (see tip box above). Thread a disc bead on to a headpin, then begin rolling the strip of paper around the headpin.

2 Brush the last 5 to 6 cm (2 to 2¼ in) of both sides of the strip with découpage medium. Finish rolling the paper and brush with a little more découpage medium to seal the join and protect the surface of the paper.

3 Thread a disc bead on to the headpin followed by a paper bead. Add a barrel bead and push the end of the roll of paper inside. Using round-nose pliers, bend the end of the headpin into a round loop that fits tightly against the barrel bead. Repeat Steps 1 to 3 to make 18 paper beads.

4 Thread as many rocailles as each safety pin can take. Thread six pins with green beads, six with blue beads and five with turquoise beads.

5 Using 5 mm jump rings, attach the paper beads to the chain, alternating with the beaded safety pins. Start at the centre and work outwards, spacing each component evenly.

6 Attach the lobster claw clasp to one end of the chain using the remaining 5 mm jump ring. Attach the 8 mm jump ring to the other end.

VARIATION
Punk pins
Safety pins are cheap and cheerful and, with the addition of beads, can be transformed into attractive charms for use in all kinds of projects. Multicoloured beads look effective – but choose any colours you wish.

tools and materials

Brocade ribbon,
37 mm (1⅜ in) wide
Scissors
Fine sewing needle
Matching sewing thread
Blue-green rocailles, size 9/0
9 blue-green leaf drops
1.3 m (4 ft 2 in) 4 mm (¼ in)
ribbon
1 cm (⅜ in) diameter button
2 × 4 mm blue-green
glass beads
2 silver calotte crimps
5 mm silver jump ring
Silver bolt ring clasp
8 mm silver jump ring
Flat-nose pliers

baroque

This neck purse features a beaded fringe and is a good way to make use of a small scrap of luxury ribbon or braid. Collectors of pretty ribbons will know that, at the luxury end, ribbon can be very expensive. So it is good to have a way to make good use of a short scrap of beautiful ribbon by making it into a little neck purse just large enough to contain a folded theatre ticket or your cab fare home.

1 Cut a 13.5 cm (5¼ in) length of ribbon and neaten each end with a narrow double hem (fold over twice and stitch). Fold the ribbon so that the lower hem is 2 cm (¾ in) from the top hem: this 2 cm (¾ in) excess will form the flap of the purse.

2 Starting at one of the bottom corners and using the thread double, slipstitch the sides together. As you do this, add the rocailles to form a border on each side of the purse and all round the flap.

3 Rejoin the thread to the bottom corner of the purse and start making a fringe. Thread on six rocailles and one leaf drop. Thread the needle back through the beads and fasten to the purse at the starting point.

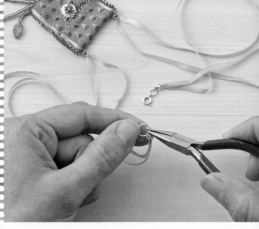

4 Bring out the needle approximately 0.5 cm (¼ in) along, thread on 14 rocailles and a leaf drop and finish as before. Make three more beaded drops, each eight beads longer than the last, then work the other side of the fringe to match.

5 Cut off 5 cm (2 in) of narrow ribbon and use this to make a button loop stitched to the underside of the flap. Stitch the button to the front of the purse, adding a cluster of rocailles.

6 Cut the remaining ribbon in half. Thread a 4 mm bead on to each piece, slip to the centre and knot in place, then stitch to the top of the purse, one at either corner. On each side, knot the two ribbon ends together and cover with a calotte. Attach a 5 mm jump ring and clasp to one and an 8 mm jump ring to the other.

The leaf drops add a nice touch to the ends of the beaded strands. A drop bead is a bead with a hole at the top. See the cluster earrings on pages 96–7 for more examples of drop beads.

tools and materials

Crochet hook, 1.75 mm
Fine cotton yarn, size 12
Scissors
Flower appliqué
Sewing needle
Matching sewing thread
50 lilac seed beads
Tiny button
Pink seed bead
10 cm (4 in) pom-pom braid

threadbare

Crochet a tiny neck purse and embellish it with beads for a necklace that is practical as well as pretty. If you can crochet, you will find this project easy. Beginners to crochet needn't be put off as you need only make a small rectangle. And knitters can knit a purse instead. Can't knit or crochet? Cut a piece from an old jumper or use a piece of ribbon or fabric.

1 Make a foundation chain of 20 and work 34 rows in double crochet (see crochet techniques on page 33).

2 **Buttonhole row:** 9 double crochet, 2 chain, miss 2 stitches on the previous row, double crochet to the end of the row. Fasten off and cut the yarn.

3 Fold the work in half to assess the position of the flower, then stitch the flower in place.

4 Thread 50 beads on to the yarn. Fold the purse in half and rejoin the yarn to the bottom right-hand corner. Join the two edges with slipstitch, working 22 stitches up the side seam to the top corner. Chain 160 to form the strap and join to the opposite top corner, then work 22 stitches down the second side seam.

5 Push the first bead up close to the corner. Slipstitch back up the side edge and the strap and down the opposite edge, pushing up one bead close to the stitch on every fifth stitch. Fasten off.

6 Stitch the button on the top front edge of the purse, opposite the buttonhole, securing it with the pink seed bead.

7 Cut a length of pom-pom braid slightly longer than the lower edge of the purse. Fold in the two ends and stitch down, then stitch the braid to the purse.

VARIATION
As this purse is made from a simple rectangular piece of crochet, it is easy to make it smaller or larger, as you please, and to vary the colours and decorations according to your whim.

32

crochet techniques

Here are the basic crochet stitches you need to make the purse on pages 30–2 or the beaded wristband on pages 88–9. Whichever crochet stitch you are working, to incorporate beads it is a simple case of slipping a bead close to the hook and continuing with the stitch.

CHAIN

Make a loop in the yarn. Insert the hook, hook it around the yarn and pull a loop through. This is one chain stitch; repeat as necessary.

DOUBLE CROCHET

Double crochet is worked into a foundation chain (a series of chain stitches) or into the loops of a previous crochet row. To make one double crochet, insert the hook into the front of the loop, hook it round the yarn and pull the loop through. There are now two loops on the hook. Wrap the yarn round the hook and pull it through both loops.

SLIPSTITCH

Insert the hook into a loop (a foundation chain or previous crochet row) and hook a loop of yarn through. Repeat on the next stitch and along the row. In this example, slipstitch is being used to join two edges together in a neat seam.

tools and materials

10 cm (4 in) scrap of leather
Ballpoint pen
Leather punch
Scissors
2.5 cm (1 in) diameter pink button
Matching thread
Beading needle
Silver calotte crimps
Flat-nose pliers
Aqua and pink farfalle beads
Silver French crimps
Fish bead
2 pink, 2 aqua flat disc beads
8 × 8 mm silver jump rings
56 cm (22 in) flat leather thong
2 silver box crimps
Silver lobster claw clasp
Short length silver chain

hunter

This pendant is made from a piece of leather, pierced and threaded with beads and suspended from a leather thong. Leather scraps are easy to come by but you needn't use the real thing if you prefer not to, as faux leather fabrics, as long as they are fray-proof, will work just as well.

Farfalle beads are an unusual shape, something like a figure of eight or a bow, with a hole in the centre, and they fit together snuggly, forming an interesting pattern. If you can't get hold of them, use any small bead instead.

34

1 Trace the template on page 110 and transfer it on to the leather. Mark holes where indicated with a ballpoint pen. Punch the holes using a leather punch, then cut out the shape.

2 Place the button in the centre of the leather shape and mark the position of the button holes. Punch these out.

3 Cut a thin sliver of leather from the offcuts about 8 cm (3¼ in) long and 2 mm (1/12 in) wide. Thread this through the holes in the leather and through the button and knot the ends to hold the button in place. Trim the ends.

4 Cut a 36 cm (14 in) length of thread, thread the beading needle and knot the strands together, about 1 cm (⅜ in) from the ends. Lay the knot inside a calotte crimp and squeeze shut with flat-nose pliers.

5 Thread 33 farfalle beads on to the needle, followed by a French crimp. Pass the needle through the hole in the fish bead, back through the crimp and several of the beads. Pull up the thread and flatten the crimp using pliers.

6 Repeat Step 5 with flat disc beads on the ends instead of the fish, and thread on fewer beads: 21 for the two end strands and 27 for the ones in between.

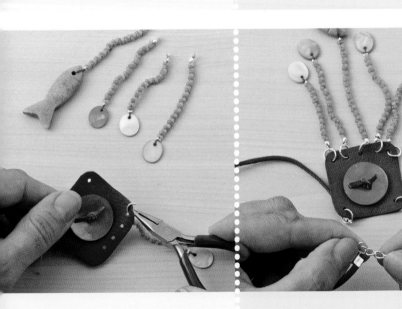

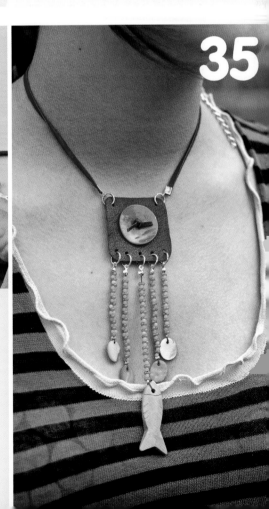

7 Attach the beaded strands to the holes in the leather using jump rings.

8 Cut the leather thong in half and attach a box crimp to either end of each piece. Add a jump ring to one end and a lobster clasp to the other. If you wish, add a short chain to allow you to adjust the length of the necklace.

75 cm (30 in) silver cord
Pink silk thread
2 silver cord ends
Flat-nose pliers
Beading needle
Seed beads in pink and lilac
Scissors
5 mm silver jump ring
Silver lobster claw clasp

beaded cord

Decorate a length of cord with beads, then add a pendant. Instructions for the beaded tassel are on pages 38–9. The combination of a twisted cord and sparkly beads creates a lovely strong base from which you can hang your choice of pendant. Cords are available in various thicknesses and colours: choose the one that appeals to you most and decorate it with your choice of beads.

36

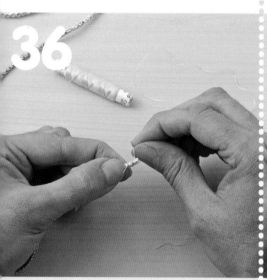

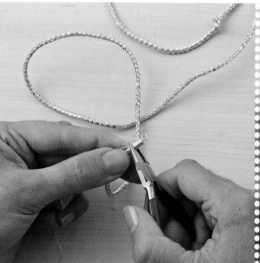

1 Bind one end of the cord tightly with thread, leaving a long end of thread.

2 Slip a cord end over the bound end of the cord and squash the last coil with flat-nose pliers to trap the cord firmly.

3 Thread the needle on to the end of the thread and add 10 seed beads. Pass the needle through the surface of the cord about 1 cm (⅜ in) along. Pull up tightly and pass the needle through the same place again to secure the beads.

4 Thread another 10 seed beads on to the needle and push the beads along the thread, ensuring that they wrap around the cord, then pass the needle through the surface of the cord 1 cm (⅜ in) from the last place. Pull up tightly and pass the needle through again to secure the beads.

5 Repeat Step 4 until you reach the end of the cord. Use any remaining thread to wrap around the cord and cover with a cord end, as before. Cut excess thread.

6 Attach a jump ring to one of the cord ends and a lobster clasp to the other.

37

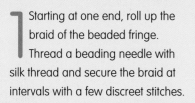

tools and materials

15 cm (6 in) purple beaded
fringe
Beading needle
Matching silk thread
Purple seed beads
Medium-size bead
Scissors

beaded tassel

This beaded tassel can be hung from the beaded cord on pages 36–7 or threaded on to a ribbon. The choice is yours. Check out your local haberdashery counter for beaded fringing. It can be expensive to buy but you only need a short length to make a tassel. Alternatively, make your own beaded fringe by stitching strands of beads on to a piece of flat braid.

1 Starting at one end, roll up the braid of the beaded fringe. Thread a beading needle with silk thread and secure the braid at intervals with a few discreet stitches.

2 Bring the needle up in the centre of the roll of braid. Thread about 10 to 12 seed beads on to the needle, then pick up a small piece of the braid at the base of the roll, close to the top of the beaded fringe. Pull up tightly.

3 Repeat Step 2 until the whole of the top of the tassel is covered with beads and the braid is no longer visible.

4 Thread a medium-size bead (use one taken from a spare piece of the fringe), then about 30 to 35 seed beads, to make a loop. Thread the needle back through the medium-size bead and secure to the top of the tassel. Trim excess thread.

tools and materials

Narrow light blue ribbon
Scissors
Silver pendant bead
2 silver box crimps
Flat-nose pliers
Light blue sewing thread
(optional)
Short length of silver link chain
Silver jump rings
Silver lobster claw clasp
Silver charm or odd earring

theatre

Show off your swan-like neck with a theatrical ribbon choker: it's the height of elegance. It's also a great way to display a pretty earring that has lost its companion. As ribbons are available in so many beautiful colours, you should have no trouble finding one to complement your choice of charm or the odd earring that no longer forms half of a matching pair. If you add a short piece of chain to one end of the ribbon, you will be able to adjust the length of the choker.

40

1 Measure around your neck and cut a length of light blue ribbon to the exact size. Slip the pendant bead on to the ribbon.

2 Clamp a box crimp to each end of the ribbon using flat-nose pliers. (You may need to bind the ribbon ends with thread first, to make it fit better inside the crimp.)

3 Add a short length of chain to one end, using a jump ring. Attach a lobster claw clasp to the other.

4 Now you can add the star attraction, using one or two jump rings, depending on the attachment on the charm.

VARIATIONS

Ooh la la
Knot a large jump ring on to the centre of a length of ribbon and use lace end crimps at either end.

Skull-and-crossbones
Your choice of 'dangle' doesn't have to be elegant or refined. A skull-and-crossbones charm can look just as effective – and perhaps more appropriate if you are attending a rock gig rather than a classical concert.

35 cm (14 in) 1 cm (¾ in) wide
blue braid
35 cm (14 in) 1 cm (¾ in) wide
pink braid
2 x 2 cm (¾ in) silver lace end
crimps
2 x 1 cm (⅜ in) silver lace end
crimps
Flat-nose pliers
Few pink and blue rocailles
Silver eyepin
Wire cutters
Round-nose pliers
Silver butterfly charm
Short length of silver chain
2 silver jump rings

butterfly

On dressing-up days, what could be prettier than a choker of flowery braid with a butterfly charm dangling from a chain? Choose braid to match or contrast with your daintiest dress and headscarf, and wait for all those admiring glances.

42

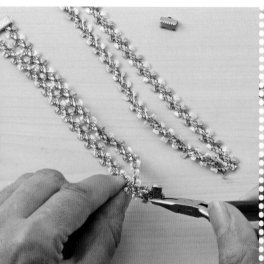

1 Cut two lengths of braid in half. Place two braid ends, one blue and one pink, next to each other in a 2 cm (¾ in) lace end crimp and press shut with flat-nose pliers.

2 Place the other ends of these braids, one on top of each other, in a 1 cm (⅜ in) lace end crimp and press shut.

3 Thread a few rocailles on to the eyepin, cut off any excess wire with wire cutters and turn the wire end into a neat loop using round-nose pliers. Attach the butterfly charm to the other end of the wire.

4 Attach a 7 cm (2¾ in) length of chain (with an odd number of links) to the two 1 cm (⅜ in) lace end crimps, using jump rings, then attach the charm to the centre link of the chain.

Choose lace end crimps in the same width as the braid or ribbon. If the crimps are a ittle bit wider, it should not matter too much; if they are narrower, pleat the ends of the ribbons slightly, to make them fit. If lace end crimps are not available, bind the ends of the ribbon and fit them into cord end crimps or box crimps. In other words, use the materials available, plus a little ingenuity.

43

tools and materials

Beading needle
Strong beading thread
2 silver French crimps (optional)
2 silver calotte crimps
Green, white and yellow rocailles
Silver lobster claw clasp
Silver jump ring

daisy chain

Reminiscent of a summer meadow, this beaded necklace will add a fresh touch to your outfit on a sunny day. There are several variations on the daisy chain, using more or fewer beads, and this is one of the simplest and most versatile. It requires a bit of patience and dexterity but you will speed up once you get the hang of it. Why not make a matching bracelet, ring and headband to complete the look?

1 Thread a beading needle with a 1.2 m (47 in) length of strong thread. Tie a knot at the end, or use a French crimp, and cover with a calotte crimp. Thread on five green rocailles, then four white, then one yellow.

2 Pass the needle back through the first white bead and push all the beads down to the end of the thread, close to the French crimp.

3 Add two more white beads and pass the needle back through the fourth white bead. This forms one flower.

VARIATIONS

Set and match

For the headband (above), flowers are made in alternate colours without extra beads in between.

For the ring, thread small beads on to nylon thread or fine elastic. Use fewer beads between each flower.

4 Thread on five green beads and repeat Steps 2 and 3. Continue repeating until you have about 12 to 15 cm (5 to 6 in) of spare thread left in the needle, or until the necklace is the desired length. Finish with five green beads.

5 Make a knot close to the final bead, or use a French crimp, and cover with a calotte crimp. Add a lobster claw clasp to one end and a jump ring to the other.

Strong medium-weight thread
Scissors
Plain and patterned
wooden beads
Assorted opaque rocailles
All-purpose glue

stranded

Single-strand necklaces combine beads of different sizes and colours for maximum impact. Try combining bright beads of different shapes and sizes into long, colourful strands. Wear one or more strands together to brighten up a plain sweater or shirt. If you can't find the beads you want, decorate your own using acrylic paints and a fine brush (see pages 48–9).

46

1 Cut a length of thread about 8 cm (3¼ in) longer than you wish the finished necklace to be. Knot a small bead on to the end, as a stopper, to prevent the other beads sliding off.

2 Start threading the beads. In this example, a small red wooden bead is threaded between every other bead to introduce an element of regularity – but you may prefer a completely random pattern.

3 When the necklace is the desired length, remove the stopper bead and knot the thread ends together.

You will not need a fastening if a necklace is long enough to pass over your head with ease. For a shorter necklace, however, add a clasp following the instructions shown on page 45.

4 Put a tiny blob of glue on the knot, to secure it.

47

Plain, unvarnished wooden beads
Toothpicks
Acrylic paints
Paintbrushes
Clear nail varnish

painted beads

Wooden beads are usually quite inexpensive – especially if you paint your own. They come in a wide range of shapes and sizes and unvarnished beads can be painted with acrylic paints – you just need a steady hand and a fine paintbrush. Skewer beads on to a wooden toothpick while you paint them, and lay the toothpicks across the neck of a jar or eggcup, or stick them into a potato or a piece of cork, while the paint dries.

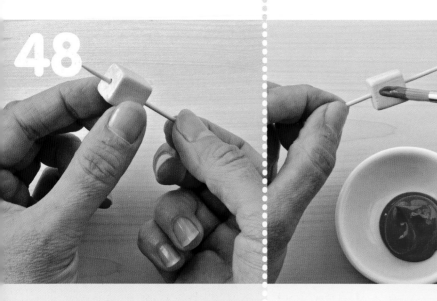

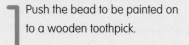

1 Push the bead to be painted on to a wooden toothpick.

2 Paint the bead all over with a base colour and leave to dry. Paint a second coat, if necessary.

3 With a contrasting colour, add a simple pattern of spots or stripes.

4 Once the paint is dry, protect the bead with a coat or two of clear varnish.

VARIATIONS
You can buy striped beads (above) – or make your own by stringing a series of flat disc beads with a half-spherical bead on either side (top left).

49

tools and materials

Shrink plastic, 13 cm (5⅛ in)
square
Pencil
Yellow, orange and light green
coloured pencils
Scissors
Hole punch
Aluminium foil
Baking tray
Domestic oven or heat tool
Orange and yellow rocailles
5 silver eyepins
Yellow flat oval disc beads
5 mm and 8 mm silver jump
rings
Brown leather thong
Silver barrel bead
2 silver cord end crimps
Flat-nose pliers

plastic fantastic

Make a necklace in a shape you like using shrink plastic
and adding a few fancy charms. The shape of this necklace
was inspired by fragments of an Iron-age harness in the
National Museum of Wales but it has been interpreted
in a more modern material. Shrink plastic, when heated,
shrinks to a seventh of its original size.

50

1 Place a sheet of shrink plastic, rough
side up, over the template on page 110
and trace the outline in pencil. Colour
in the shape using the coloured pencils.
Colour in lightly, as the colour will intensify
as the plastic shrinks. Don't worry if you go
over the lines, as the shape will be cut out.
Cut around the outlines and cut out the
central shape.

2 Punch out the holes with the hole
punch. Place on a foil-lined
baking tray and, following the
manufacturer's instructions, place in
the oven for a few minutes (or use a
heat tool). The shape will shrink, curl up,
then begin to flatten. As soon as this
happens, remove from the oven and
place a flat, heavy object on top.

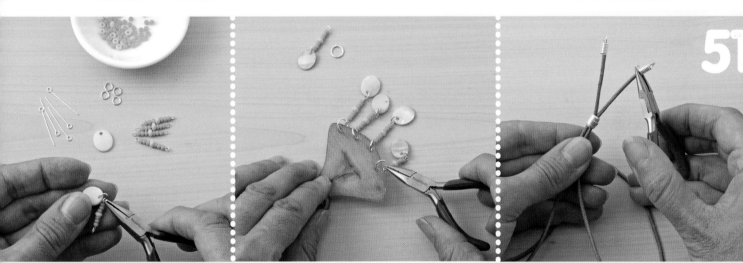

3 Thread three orange, one yellow and three more orange rocaille beads on to an eyepin and attach a disc bead to the eyepin, using a 5 mm jump ring. Make four more dangles in the same way.

4 Attach the five beaded dangles, using 8 mm jump rings, to the holes at the bottom of the shape.

5 Push the ends of the thong into a barrel bead, then into two cord end crimps and squash the last coil with flat-nose pliers to hold in place. Attach the cord ends to the top of the pendant, using 8 mm jump rings.

brooches & pins

tools and materials

Scraps of silk, chiffon or
organza
Embroidery scissors
A few lengths of metallic silver
thread
2 mm (½₂ in) wide yellow
embroidery ribbon
Stamens
Hot glue gun
Hatpin

pom-pom

Made from fragments of silk fabrics and threads, this gorgeous creation can be worn on your lapel, in your hair, on a hat... and why stop at one? Search your scrap bag for suitable fabrics — silks, chiffon and organza are ideal as they are fine-textured and liable to fraying, which enhances the finished effect. The stamens used here can be found in shops that specialise in flower crafts or bridal favours.

> If you prefer, you can glue the bundle to a brooch pin or hair slide instead.
> Use the ends of the ribbon to wrap around the bar of the pin or slide, for extra security.

54

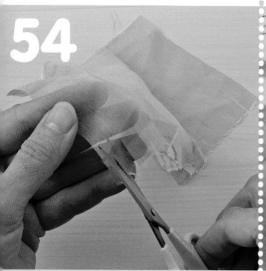

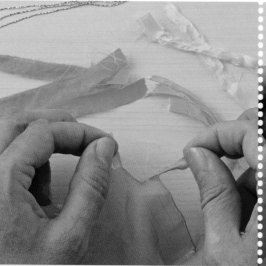

1 Cut strips of fabric 9 cm (3½ in) wide. Snip into the long edge at approximately 1 cm (⅜ in) intervals using sharp embroidery scissors.

2 Tear the fabric into strips along the snips. Use at least three different fabrics, preferably more. Cut 9 cm (3½ in) lengths of metallic thread, too.

3 Cut a 30 cm (12 in) length of embroidery ribbon and lay it vertically on the work surface. Lay fabric strips and threads across it. When you have built up a bundle of strips and threads, add a few stamens and tie the bundle tightly around the middle, with the ribbon.

4 Place a blob of glue in the centre of the knot, place the blunt end of the hatpin on top and quickly fold the bundle in half, to enclose the top of the pin. Hold for a few moments until the glue sets.

5 Trim the pom-pom to an even shape. Take care not to snip off the stamens.

55

medal

Papier mâché is a great recycling craft, making excellent use of old newspapers. This is an unusual but very effective choice for jewellery-making – but not suitable for wet weather wear. Hunt for eye-catching pictures from magazines or wrapping paper to feature on your medal. It could be a picture of a movie star, a vintage comic cutout or a word or phrase that gets your message across.

56

1 Cut two 5 cm (2 in) circles from scrap card. Open out a paper clip and bend it back and forth until it snaps in half. Lay it flat down the centre of one of the card shapes with a loop protruding from the bottom and tape in place. Glue the two card shapes together with the paper clip sandwiched in between.

2 Now cover the circles with two or three layers of papier mâché. To do this, brush découpage medium on to torn strips of newspaper and lay them on to the card, smoothing them down. Pay particular attention to covering the edges of the circle. Hang up to dry, using the paper clip loop.

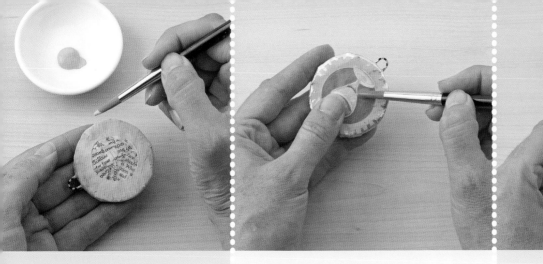

3 Paint the edges and front border yellow. Paint the central area orange.

4 Paste your chosen picture on to the front of the badge. When the glue is dry, use the silver paint pen to outline the edge. Give the brooch a hardwearing finish by brushing with one or two coats of découpage medium or clear nail varnish.

5 As a finishing touch, glue on a jewel (or two or more), then glue the brooch pin to the back of the brooch using all-purpose glue – or use a self-adhesive pin like the one shown here.

6 Attach a few charms to the paper clip with a large jump ring.

VARIATIONS

Happy

Follow the same method but use a paper cutout of a clown, adding a red jewelled nose. Suspend a disc with beaded dangles from the base of the brooch and finish with touches of green and silver glitter.

Good girl

You can cut the card base to any simple shape – such as a heart. This version has a gold border and plenty of jewels and glitter.

tools and materials

Scrap card (from a
cardboard box)
Scissors
Metal bottle tops
All-purpose glue or
hot-melt glue gun
Printed pictures
Paper adhesive
3D embossing liquid
Pin, just in case
Small brooch pin

badges

Badges are the favoured decoration on lapels the world over, featuring slogans, graphics and pop star portraits, among other things. As well as being decorative, the ubiquitous lapel pin has been used for decades to proclaim allegiance to various causes, as a tool of propaganda and to advertise products. Market stalls, clothing stores and record shops offer vast selections and though they are cheap and plentiful, you may just yearn to make your own. So here is a method where you don't need a special badge-making machine, just a collection of bottle tops.

1 Cut circles of card to fit easily inside the bottle tops. It doesn't matter if they are slightly smaller. Glue them in place using all-purpose glue or a hot-melt glue gun.

2 Cut pictures from magazines or brochures to fit and glue them in place using paper adhesive.

3 Flood the inside of the bottle tops with 3D embossing liquid until the picture is completely covered. If there are any bubbles, burst them with a pin immediately. Leave to dry to a clear, glass-like finish. Attach a brooch pin to the back of each one.

tools and materials

Scrap of medium-weight non-woven interfacing
Scissors
Ballpoint pen
Beading needle
Strong sewing thread
Yellow, turquoise, orange, green and white rocailles
Fabric glue
Scrap of leather or felt
Brooch pin

native

Reminiscent of Native American beadwork, this brooch would look equally good on the prairie or on a city street. A brooch thickly encrusted with beads looks impressive but is really straightforward to make. Once you have got the hang of it, you can easily come up with your own designs.

1 Cut a 7 cm (2¾ in) square of interfacing. Place it on top of the template on page 110 and trace the design, using a ballpoint pen.

2 Thread a beading needle with strong sewing thread. Starting in the centre of the design, stitch on yellow rocailles individually to fill the central shape. Then outline this with a single row of turquoise beads.

3 Continue in this way until all the areas of the design have been filled, with orange beads for the petals and green for the leaves.

VARIATIONS

Colourful

Make matching rings in a similar way (shown right), using just the centre of the motif and gluing it on to a ring base with a flat plate.

Choose your own colour scheme, using at least five different colours and adding a contrasting border around the edge of the brooch, if you like.

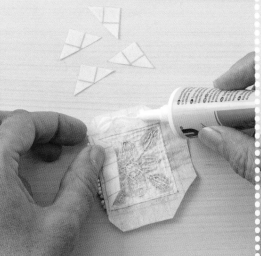

4 Fill in the background with white beads until the whole area has been filled.

5 Cut off the corners of the interfacing and fold all four sides to the back, gluing them in place with a little fabric glue.

6 Cut a 4 cm (1½ in) square of leather or felt and glue in place to cover the back of the brooch, then stitch (or glue) a brooch pin in place.

tools and materials

Fine silver wire
Blue and green size 8/0 rocailles
Flat-nose pliers
Medium-sized round yellow bead
Florists' tape
Brooch pin

flower power

This flower, fashioned from beaded petals and leaves, is perfect for stitching to a hat or handbag, or pinning to your jacket lapel. The petals of this flower, made from small glass beads, will catch the light beautifully. When choosing the central bead, bear in mind that the hole in the centre will have to accommodate 12 strands of wire.

1 Cut a 60 cm (2 ft) length of fine silver wire. Thread on seven blue rocailles and push them to the centre of the wire. Pass one end of the wire back through the last four beads and pull tightly. Use flat-nose pliers to pull the wire, if necessary.

2 Thread five more rocailles on to one end of the wire and pass the other end back through the five beads. Pull up tightly, again using pliers if you need to.

3 Now thread on six rocailles, passing both wires through the beads from opposite directions, as before. Continue, adding a row of seven beads, then eight, then six, then five, then four, then three – this forms one petal. Make five more petals in the same way. Make two more using green beads, for the leaves.

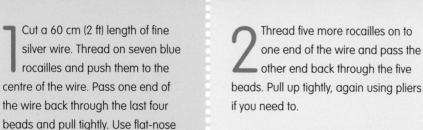

4 Pass the ends of the wires from all petals through the yellow bead and back around the outside of the bead, gathering them together and twisting them to form a stem.

5 Start binding the top of the stem with florists' tape. Pass the tape over the bar of the brooch pin, binding the pin firmly to the stem.

6 Add the leaves, binding their stems together with the main flower stem.

VARIATION

Stamens

Use beads of any colour to make the flower petals. In this example, instead of being used to form a stem, some of the wire ends have been pushed back up through the central bead to form stamens and the remaining pieces of wire used to attach a brooch pin to the reverse.

Strong beading thread
Scissors
Beading needle
2.5 cm (1 in) diameter
perforated metal disc
Turquoise, cream, blue and
brown ceramic beads
3 tubular beads
Brooch pin
Flat-backed gemstone
Metal adhesive

noble

This round brooch with beaded drops would look good as a fastening for a scarf or cloak. A clever technique is used to form the border – carefully follow the step-by-step instructions and the result is very impressive. The beads used here are made of ceramic. Any small beads will do, however: choose your own selection of four different colours.

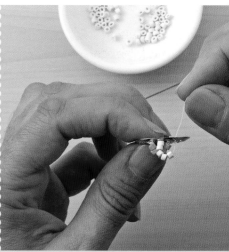

1 Cut a 70 cm (28 in) length of beading thread. Thread the needle and fasten one end to the perforated disc. Bring the needle to the front through one of the holes on the outer row and thread on five turquoise beads.

2 Skip one hole and pass the needle through the next hole to the back. Pull the thread tight. The beads will form a small arch.

3 Bring the needle up through the hole you have skipped, between the two holes occupied by the strand of turquoise beads. Thread five cream beads on to the needle, pass the needle down through the next-but-one hole along and pull the thread tight.

4 Now bring the needle up through the next hole, thread with five blue beads and pass down through the next free hole, next to the strand of cream beads. Continue in this way, with five brown beads next, until you have gone all the way round the edge of the disc and back to the beginning.

5 Pass the needle through one of the beads at the very edge of the disc, through a tubular bead, then a small bead, back through the tubular bead and the small bead on the edge, to the back of the brooch. Repeat twice more.

6 Use the remaining thread to stitch the brooch pin in place, then glue the flat-backed gem in the centre of the brooch using metal adhesive.

VARIATION
Bright as a button

Using exactly the same technique but with colourful opaque rocailles, you can make a brooch with a totally different character. In this case, a bright button has been used to fill the central space.

65

charmed, i'm sure

This quirky pin displays a random selection of charms, beads and buttons of different shapes, sizes and colours. Use this as an opportunity to display your own unique collection of quirky and colourful charms. Some bead suppliers have a selection of charms for sale but you could also use tiny plastic novelties from crackers, small toys, broken earrings and odd buttons. Some collectors sell charms via the internet: type the phrase 'crackerjack prizes' or 'gumball charms' into the search engine and see what comes up.

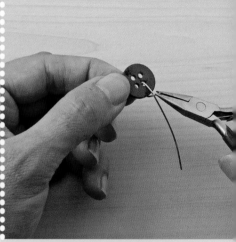

1 Prepare the charms by attaching a jump ring to each. You will probably find 5 mm jump rings most useful and unobtrusive for this.

2 Attach a few of the charms to short lengths (about 4 cm/1½ in) of fine chain, again using 5 mm jump rings.

3 You can include buttons, which are cheap and cheerful, by using a length of wire to create a hanging loop.

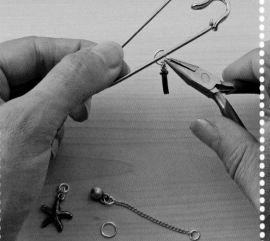

4 Make simple dangles by threading seed beads on to headpins and, using round-nose pliers, turning the end of the pin into a loop.

5 Use an 8 mm jump ring to attach each charm to the kilt pin. Make sure you attach them to the static bar of the pin and not to the side that opens.

6 Continue attaching charms until you are happy with the result. Then place an 8 mm jump ring on the bar between each of the rings holding the charms. This fills up excess space and helps to prevent all the charms from sliding to one end of the pin.

VARIATIONS
Loopy pins

Instead of a plain pin, look for pins with integral rings or loops, specially designed for adding charms. One of these brooches has a rock 'n' roll theme while the other has been decorated with big and small star charms.

tools and materials

Picture of your choice
Glue stick
Scrap of thin card
Pen or pencil
Acetate
Scissors
Transparent self-adhesive film
Sharp darning needle
Flat-nose pliers
Beading needle
Strong beading thread
All-purpose glue
Assortment of beads, including
seed beads and rocailles
Brooch pin

pin-up

Wear a picture of your idol on your lapel – or choose any picture to express your mood, style or opinion. This project employs a very low-tech method of laminating, involving acetate and sticky-backed plastic. If you prefer, you can get your picture heat laminated at your local copy shop. Any picture will do for this project, as long as the surface is smooth and flat, and not textured. Rather than cut up an original, it's a good idea to get a colour photocopy done for this purpose.

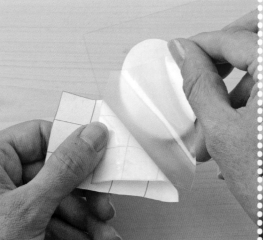

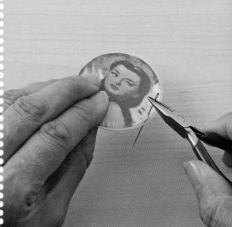

68

1 Stick your chosen picture on to thin card. Trace the oval shape from page 110 and use it to cut a template from acetate. Place this acetate template on top of your picture and draw around the outline. Cut out.

2 Place the cutout picture face-down on a piece of acetate. Peel off the backing paper from a piece of self-adhesive film and stick it over the back of the picture. Burnish the film so it sticks firmly. Cut out around the picture, leaving a 3 mm (⅛ in) margin. The picture is now protected front and back.

3 Now, using the darning needle and flat-nose pliers to help you, pierce evenly-spaced holes about 0.5 cm (¼ in) apart, around the margin of the picture.

4 Thread the beading needle with strong thread and knot the end. Pass the needle up through one of the holes and back down through an adjacent hole, then through the knot to secure it (for added security, dab the knot with a blob of glue). Bring the needle back to the front and thread on four beads.

5 Pass the needle down through the adjacent hole. Continue to do this until you have created an inner border of beads.

6 Now thread a slightly larger bead and eight smaller beads, then another slightly larger bead on to the needle. Bring the needle up through the adjacent hole from the back and pass it back through the last medium bead, to create a loop. Repeat all round. Glue the brooch pin to the back.

It is surprising what different effects you can achieve with various pictures and combinations of beads. Bugles, discs, rocailles and seed beads can all be used to good effect.

tools and materials

Pictures to copy
Inkjet/laser transfer paper
Scissors
Scrap of white fine-weave
cotton fabric
Iron
Sewing needle
White cotton thread
Oddments of ribbon
Buttons or beads (optional)
Safety pins

patches

Picture perfect patches can be pinned to jackets, jeans, bags, hats and so on for an instant style statement. These fabric patches can feature your own selection of pictures or messages. They can be pinned to your clothes or attached with Velcro, poppers or buttons but if you want to make them more permanent, stitch them securely in place. To make the photo transfer, you will need a sheet of transfer paper: various brands are available, for either inkjet or laser printers and copiers.

1 Print or photocopy your picture on to the transfer paper. Follow the manufacturer's instructions and make sure you print a mirror image of the photograph or the original will be reversed when you come to transfer it to the fabric.

2 Trim the transfer, leaving a thin white margin all around, if possible. Place face-down on to a clean, dry, laundered piece of white cotton fabric and press with a hot iron for 2 minutes (or according to manufacturer's instructions). Leave to cool, then carefully peel away the backing fabric.

3 Trim the fabric to leave a 2 cm (¾ in) wide border.

4 Turn under the raw edges to form a narrow double hem and stitch in place with running stitch.

5 Add a border of narrow ribbon and stitch on a few buttons or beads, if you wish. The patch is now ready to be pinned or stitched on to your clothes.

Medium-weight interfacing,
self-adhesive or heat fusible

Scissors

Scrap of cotton fabric with
a small print

Sewing needle

Matching pale pink and white
sewing thread

Image transferred to white
fabric (see box)

12 cm (5 in) green and white
narrow lace trim

15 cm (6 in) pale pink fine
ric-rac braid

4 doll-sized buttons

4 rocailles

10 cm (4 in) 0.5 cm (¼ in) peach
ribbon

Large safety pin

8 cm (3¼ in) pink edging braid

8 cm (3¼ in) of 3.5 cm (1⅜ in)
ribbon

fabrication

Have fun creating this fabric brooch suspended from a safety pin. Made from scraps, there is lots of scope for personalisation. Once you have mastered the basic principles of creating a brooch like this, raid your workbox for suitable materials. The tiniest scraps of fabric, lace and braid, odd buttons, sequins and beads can all be used.

Transfer your choice of image on to white cotton fabric using an iron-on transfer material. Various brands are available: make sure you choose one suitable for the type of printer or photocopier you are using, either inkjet or laser.

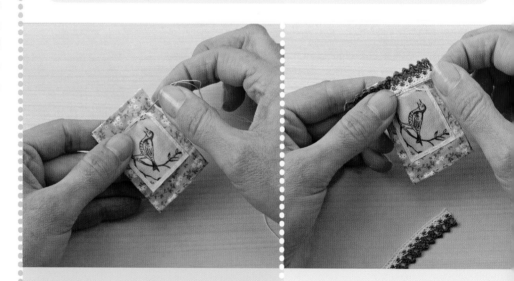

1 Cut a 4 x 6 cm (1½ x 2¼ in) rectangle of interfacing and apply it to the back of the fabric. Trim the fabric to give a margin of 1.5 cm (⅝ in) all round, then fold this to the back and baste with small stitches. Trim the margin of fabric around the transferred image to 2 mm (¹⁄₁₆ in). Position the image in the centre of the fabric and stitch in place using small basting stitches.

2 Cut two lengths of lace trim and stitch in place on either side of the central image. Fold the raw ends to the back and secure with a few stitches.

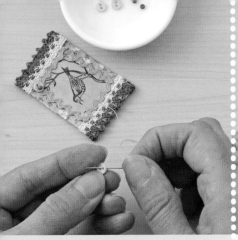

3 Stitch the ric-rac all round the central image, to form a border. Stitch a button to each corner, held in place with a rocaille.

4 Cut three short lengths of ribbon and loop them over the non-opening bar of the safety pin. Stitch the ends to the back of the brooch, close to the upper edge.

5 Stitch the edging braid to the lower edge, then fold under the two cut ends of the wide ribbon and stitch the ribbon in place to cover the back of the brooch, hiding all the stitching and untidy ends of ribbon and braid.

VARIATION

From the heart

Instead of using a photo transfer, use lace, ricrac braid and different fabrics, with some decorative stitching and sequins. Stitch a brooch pin to the back.

bracelets

tools and materials

8 mm silver jump rings
18 cm (7 in) silver flat link chain
5 mm silver jump rings
Bolt ring clasp
Flat-nose pliers
Round-nose pliers
0.6 mm silver-plated brass wire
Wire cutters
About 15 to 20 assorted buttons

buttons

This is a cute variation on the classic charm bracelet, using an assortment of buttons – making it fairly cheap to make, as well as very individual. If you haven't got your own button box, now is the time to start one – or to raid someone else's. Buttons have great character and charm and, what's more, they are as cheap as anything: you can pick them up in jumble sales and markets, or search down the back of the sofa or in an untidy drawer.

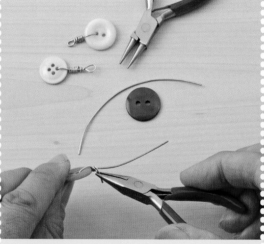

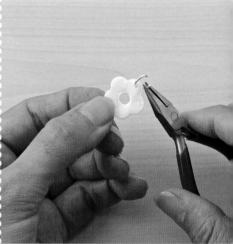

1 Attach an 8 mm jump ring to one end of the chain and use a 5 mm jump ring to attach a bolt ring to the other end.

2 Cut a 7.5 cm (3 in) length of wire. Push one end through one of the holes in the button and bend about 1 cm (⅜ in) from the end using flat-nose pliers. The place at which you bend the wire will depend on the size of the button: the short end of the wire should protrude beyond the button's edge. Bend the other end into a loop using round-nose pliers.

3 If you use a button or other flat decoration which has a hole near the edge, you can dispense with the wire and use a jump ring of the appropriate size to link it to the chain.

4 Lay out the chain and the prepared buttons and decide on your preferred sequence. Attach each button to the chain using 5 mm jump rings and spacing the buttons evenly along the links.

VARIATION
Quick fix

Here's a quick and easy idea using two-hole buttons: thread them on to beading elastic, bringing the elastic up from the back through one of the holes, back down through the other hole, then through the next button in the same way to create a double layer of buttons sitting back-to-back.

tools and materials

Beading or fine sewing needle
Strong thread
Scissors
10 small silver crimp beads
2 x 5-hole silver end bars
Flat-nose pliers
Blue bugle beads
Red seed beads
3 x 5-hole silver spacer bars
Jump rings: 1 x 5 mm, 1 x 8 mm
Silver bolt ring clasp

spaced

This stranded bead bracelet will appeal to those of you who prefer something dainty to adorn your wrist. You will need to pay a visit to your local jewellery making suppliers, either in person or online, to buy the spacer bars and end bars on which this design depends. The bracelet shown here uses bars with five holes; you can buy them with more or fewer holes for different effects. Once you get the knack of multi-stranding using spacer bars, you could try your hand at bracelets of varying widths, using all kinds of different beads. You could even make a matching choker.

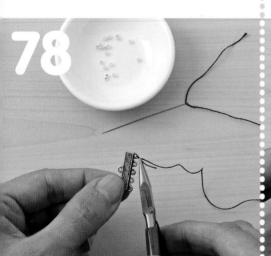

1 Thread a needle with 30 cm (12 in) of strong thread. Pass it through a crimp bead, then through the first loop on one of the end bars and back through the crimp. Slide the crimp close to the bar, leaving a short tail of thread, then squeeze the crimp flat with flat-nose pliers.

2 Thread the first bugle bead on to the needle and push it up close to the crimp, trying to ensure that the tail of thread goes through the bead. Trim the thread close to the bead.

3 Proceed with threading the beads – bugles alternating with seed beads – for 3.5 cm (1⅜ in) or, in this case, six of each bead, then pass the needle through the first hole in a spacer bar.

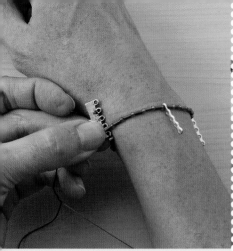

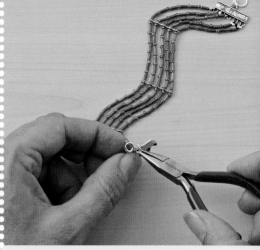

4 Thread on more beads – the same number as in the first section – and another spacer, and repeat until you have four groups of beads and three spacers. Try it on your wrist, to make sure it is long enough.

5 Thread on a crimp bead, pass the needle through the corresponding loop on the second end bar, back through the crimp and through the first few beads so that the end of the thread will be hidden inside the beads. Squeeze the crimp flat and trim off the thread end.

6 When you have completed all five rows of beads, attach an 8 mm jump ring to one end bar, and a bolt ring clasp attached with a 5 mm jump ring to the other.

VARIATION
Mix and match
Use the same colour sequence of beads on a pair of earrings, using headpins instead of thread. These earrings (pictured right) feature a triangular support with five holes from which to hang the beaded pins. Attach them to ear wires (like the ball wires used here) or clips if you don't have pierced ears.

Linen shirt cuff
Scissors
White sewing thread
Crewel needle
Clear glass seed beads
Mother-of-pearl button
Doll-sized button
Pale blue and pink embroidery
thread
Small scraps of printed fabric
Seed beads in assorted colours
Beading needle

linen

Bare wrists are boring. Cut the cuffs from your unwanted shirts and transform them into a chic fashion statement. What you need for this project is an old shirt, or one whose sleeves need shortening – because even when you have cut off the cuffs, the shirt can surely still be worn? Meanwhile, transform the cuffs into a unique piece of arm adornment. Lighter than a bracelet – and warmer, too – this chic cuff could catch on in a big way.

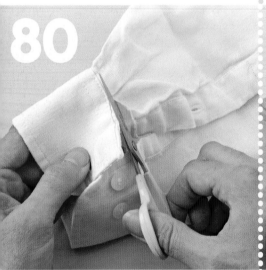

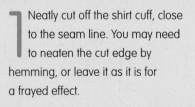

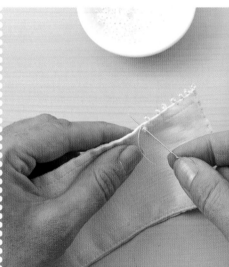

1 Neatly cut off the shirt cuff, close to the seam line. You may need to neaten the cut edge by hemming, or leave it as it is for a frayed effect.

2 Try it on for size. Your cuff is likely to be a little loose; if so, cut off a piece from the button end, to ensure a good but not too tight fit. Turn under the raw edges and slipstitch along the folds.

3 Stitch a line of clear seed beads, evenly spaced, around the edges of the cuff. On the cut edge you may want to arrange the beads quite close together in order to disguise any frayed edges.

4 Use the button you have cut off, or replace it with a new one. For a pretty effect, stitch a tiny, doll-sized button on top of a mother-of-pearl one.

5 Now use your creativity to decorate the cuff. Start by embroidering a few lines of running stitch, if you like. Use one or two strands of embroidery thread in your needle.

6 Cut out small motifs from printed fabric and sew in place, turning raw edges under with the point of the needle as you stitch. Then add a border of seed beads around each stitched motif and a few clusters of beads in between.

VARIATION
Woolly warmer

Why stop at linen cuffs? This cuff was once part of a wool jacket and has been decorated with crewelwork motifs, machine stitching and shiny red seed beads.

Sheet of paper with printed text
3–5 cm (1¼–2 in) wide plastic
bangle
Découpage medium
Fine paintbrush
Sheet of butterfly print gift wrap
Small scissors
Green tissue paper or
handmade paper

flutter

Use découpage finish to give bargain bangles from a boot sale or the bottom of a drawer a whole new lease of life. The foundation for this project is a plain plastic bangle. You may well have something suitable knocking around at home; if not, chances are you'll find a cheap bangle or two in a thrift shop. Any width will do – as long as it is not too narrow to display your chosen cutout paper motif.

Découpage medium is a ready-mixed all-in-one water-based glaze that acts as both adhesive and varnish – perfect for a project like this. Alternatively you could use PVA glue diluted to the consistency of thin cream.

82

1 Tear the text paper into thin strips; the length should be twice the width of the bracelet. Glue these to completely cover the bracelet, laying each strip across the width and overlapping the ends on the inside.

2 While the glue is drying, cut individual motifs from wrapping paper and set aside.

3 Cut or tear narrow strips from green tissue paper and glue them on to the bracelet to form stripes, allowing glimpses of the text paper to show through.

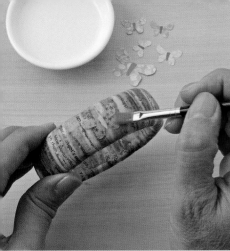

4 Now glue the butterfly motifs in place and brush plenty of découpage medium all over the surface of the paper. Apply several more coats of the product, allowing it to dry between coats, for a glossy finish.

The basic paper covering for the bangle can be a sheet torn from a phone book. For the motifs, find a sheet of wrapping paper with pretty motifs such as butterflies or flowers. When covering the bangles, it is best to tear the paper into strips, which helps to create a smoother surface, rather than cutting it. You will, however, have to cut the motifs and for this you will need a small, sharp pair of scissors with pointed blades.

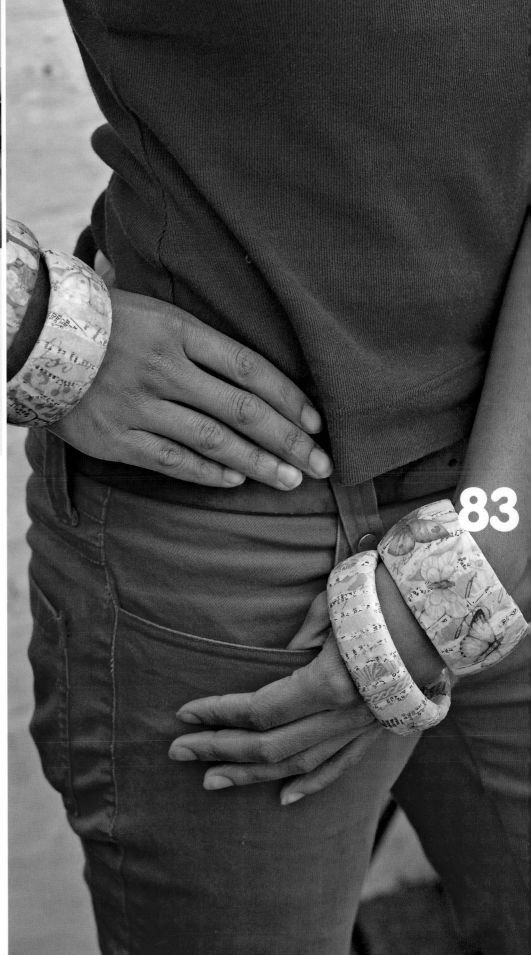

83

tools and materials

Strong silver embroidery
or crochet thread
Crochet hook, 0.75 mm
or 1.00 mm
Scissors
Needle
3 mm silver beads
11 mm mother-of-pearl button
Silver charm (optional)

metallica

This multi-strand bracelet has a clever closure made from crocheted metallic yarn. Crochet skills come to the fore again with this simple bracelet. Metallic yarn and metallic beads are perfect partners but coloured yarn and matching or contrasting coloured beads could look just as effective. See what yarn you have to hand and partner it with your own choice of beads for a uniquely pretty bracelet.

84

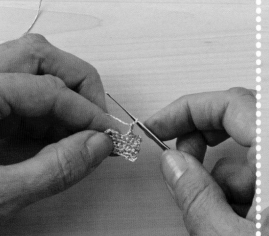

1 Using the silver embroidery thread, make 8 chain and work 4 rows in double crochet (refer to the crochet techniques on page 33, if you need to).

2 Work a buttonhole row: 3 double crochet, 2 chain, miss 2 stitches on the previous row, 3 double crochet. Fasten off the yarn. Make another piece in the same way but instead of a buttonhole row, simply work a fifth row of double crochet. Fasten off, leaving a 1.6 m (1.7 yd) length of yarn.

3 Thread the needle on to the yarn and thread on about 48 silver beads to make a 14.5 cm (5¾ in) strand. Use any needle, as long as it is fine enough to pass through the beads but with an eye large enough to accommodate the thread.

4 Pass the needle through the corner of the other piece of crochet (on the edge opposite the buttonhole), pull up tightly so the beads touch the edge, and pass the needle through the same point again, to make it secure.

5 Pass the needle through the next chain in the row and thread on another 48 silver beads. Pass the needle through the second stitch of the other crochet piece. Continue like this until you have 8 rows of beads.

6 Stitch the button in the centre of the crochet and add a silver charm if you wish.

tools and materials

Elastic cord
Scissors
At least 13 to 15 large beads,
(1–2 cm/⅜–¾ in) in size
About 30 to 35
medium-sized beads
About 13 to 15 small beads
Silver headpins
Round-nose pliers
5 mm silver jump rings
Flat-nose pliers
All-purpose glue

chunky

This bold bracelet is satisfyingly heavy and jingly to wear and will appeal to those of you who like to make a statement. It is also a good way to combine odd beads – this is your chance to use an interesting assortment of shapes and colours. Often, when buying beads, it is difficult to make a choice. With this bracelet, you can choose them all: or at least one of each of a number of interesting specimens.

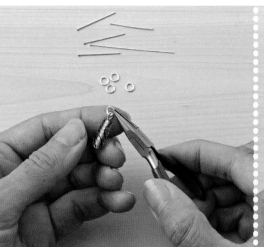

1 Cut a length of elastic cord about 10 cm (4 in) longer than the finished bracelet. Check that the large beads have holes big enough to be threaded straight on to the elastic.

2 Smaller beads, or long shapes, should be threaded on to a headpin. Use round-nose pliers to twist the headpin into a loop. Add a jump ring to the loop.

3 If the bead to be threaded on to a headpin has a large hole, slip a small bead on to the headpin first so that the bead doesn't slip off the end.

VARIATION

Ivory

If you want a more subtle effect, choose beads of one colour. This ivory-coloured bracelet has been made in the same way but without the multicoloured madness.

4 Thread your bead selection on to the elastic cord, alternating large beads with beads threaded on to headpins. When you are happy with the arrangement – and when it fits comfortably around your wrist – knot the ends of the elastic and trim off the excess. Add a dot of glue to secure.

87

tools and materials

4-ply baby pink cotton yarn
3.00 mm crochet hook
Button with shank
Beading needle or fine sewing
needle
Strong matching sewing thread
Mixture of seed beads and
bugle beads in an assortment
of sizes and colours

rococo

This richly encrusted wristband looks beautiful on a bare arm and will add a touch of sparkle to a dull day. Sometimes beads collect in the bottom of your bead box, or often there are a few beads left over from a project. Now is the time to gather together all those odd beads and use them all in one project. Of course, you may not wish to be so random, in which case you could select a special combination of different beads. That said, the success of this project probably relies on a lack of planning!

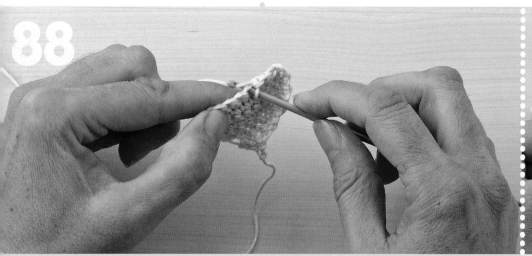

1 Firstly, make the wristband, using the four-ply cotton yarn, as follows (refer to the crochet techniques on page 33 if necessary):
Row 1: chain 3, 1 double crochet in 1st chain; turn.
Row 2: 2 chain, 1 double crochet in 1st stitch, 2 double crochet in 2nd stitch; turn.
Row 3: 2 chain, 1 double crochet in 1st stitch, 1 double crochet in each stitch to last stitch, 2 double crochet in last stitch; turn.
Repeat the last row twice, then work 32 rows of 10 double crochet without further shaping. To make the buttonhole end, decrease 1 stitch on each end of the next three rows, then make a 4-chain loop and fasten off.

2 Stitch a button on to the point opposite the button loop. Darn in the yarn ends.

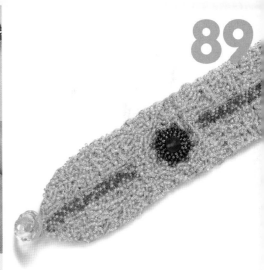

3 Thread a beading needle or fine sewing needle with a double length of thread. Start stitching rows of beads along the length of the crocheted piece. The rows don't have to be straight: in fact, the more random, the better.

4 Be sure to avoid stitching beads too close to the button loop. Continue stitching beads close together until the whole surface is thickly encrusted.

VARIATION
Planet
Instead of multi-coloured beads, transparent seed beads have been used here, with a pattern of blue and pink beads cutting a swathe through the centre.

earrings

tools and materials

Scrap of card (from
a cardboard box)
Pencil
Scissors
4 short silver eyepins
Metal glue
Newspaper
Découpage medium
Fine paintbrushes
Acrylic paints
Clear nail varnish
Short pins
Smallish beads
Seed beads
6 silver headpins
Round-nose pliers
2 x 5 mm silver jump rings
2 small buttons or charms
(see note)
2 silver earring posts

dotty

Though these earrings are really big and bold, they are
light to wear as they are made from papier mâché. The
templates for the earrings can be found on page 110.
Simply trace them on to card and cut them out, then
cover with papier mâché. Easy! Once you get the hang
of it you can run riot, making papier mâché earrings in
all shapes, sizes and colours.

1 Trace the templates on page 110 and
cut two shapes from scrap card.

2 Insert an eyepin into the top
and bottom of each shape,
having first dipped the end of
each pin into metal glue.

3 Now cover the card shapes with two or three layers of papier mâché. To do this, brush découpage medium on to torn strips of newspaper and lay them on to the card, smoothing them down. Pay particular attention to covering the edges of the card. Hang up to dry.

4 Paint the shapes all over with pink acrylic paint, then leave to dry.

5 Paint white spots on the front of each earring and, when these are dry, paint pale green spots on top. (Here, the green paint has been mixed to match the beads).

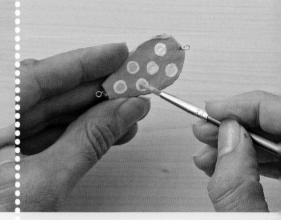

The top part of the earring is made from a plastic shape glued to the flat part of an earring post. Choose a button, charm or other item that has a hole through which you can insert a jump ring, so the bottom part of the earring can be attached.

6 Paint a border, if you wish, then add a protective coat or two of nail varnish. Thread beads on to pins, then dip the point of each pin into metal glue before inserting into the edge of the shape, evenly spaced all round.

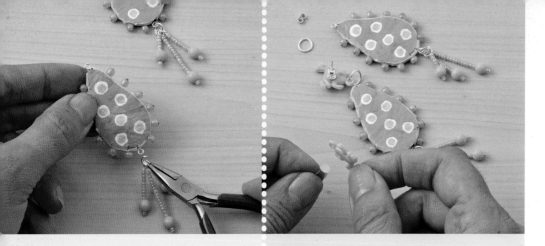

7 Thread a selection of beads on to six headpins. Use round-nose pliers to twist the top of each headpin into a loop. Thread three beaded headpins on to a 5 mm jump ring and join the jump ring to the loop at the base of the earring. Repeat for the other earring.

8 Glue a button or charm to each earring post. Leave until the glue sets, then attach the top of the earrings to the button or charm using a jump ring.

VARIATIONS

Teddy bear
You can make these earrings any colour you like – it's just a case of mixing paint. These are suspended from yellow plastic flower charms and feature faux jewels and plastic teddy charms.

Sunny
The bright colour scheme of yellow, red and white will brighten the dullest day and cheer you up when you're feeling blue.

94

tools and materials

Short length of silver chain
2 silver ear wires
5 mm silver jump rings
30 silver headpins
Small turquoise plastic faceted beads
Teardrop-shaped yellow beads
Wire cutters
Round-nose pliers
Flat-nose pliers

cascade

This clever technique creates an opulent effect, using a cluster of teardrop-shaped beads in acid yellow. Lightweight plastic beads are an ideal choice for this project, to avoid the finished earrings being too heavy. Though fiddly to make, they are very easy and the effect is impressive and very eye-catching.

1 Cut two short lengths of chain, each consisting of about 8 links, one for each earring. Loop one end of each on to ear wires, or use 5 mm jump rings to attach the chains to the ear wires.

2 Thread a small turquoise bead on to a headpin, followed by one of the larger teardrop-shaped beads. Snip off any excess wire from the headpin with wire cutters, if necessary, leaving about 1 cm (⅜ in).

3 Using round-nose pliers, make a closed loop at the end of the wire. Make 30 'dangles' – 15 for each earring – in this way.

4 Attach the first dangle to the end link of the chain, using a jump ring.

5 Attach two dangles to the next link up, each with a jump ring.

6 Continue adding 2 dangles to each link, working your way up the chain.

tools and materials

0.6 mm silver-plated brass wire
Wire cutters
Round-nose pliers
4 pink seed beads
2 barrel-shaped beads
Flat-nose pliers
3 mm silver jump rings
2 small flower charms
2 silver ear wires

east end

The simplest earrings are formed from bead droplets on silver wires. By linking separate components, they swing and sway as you move, allowing the sparkly beads to catch the light.

This method of creating beaded links is very useful for all kinds of jewellery-making. The success of the technique lies in creating neat closed loops at the ends of the wires. Practice makes perfect.

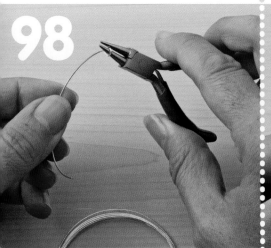

1 Cut a length of wire about 8 cm (3¼ in) with wire cutters and make a closed loop at one end using round-nose pliers.

2 Slip on two pink seed beads, trim the wire to about 1 cm (⅜ in) and make a second closed loop.

3 In a similar way, make a loop at one end of the remaining wire, slip on a barrel-shaped bead, trim the wire and make a second closed loop.

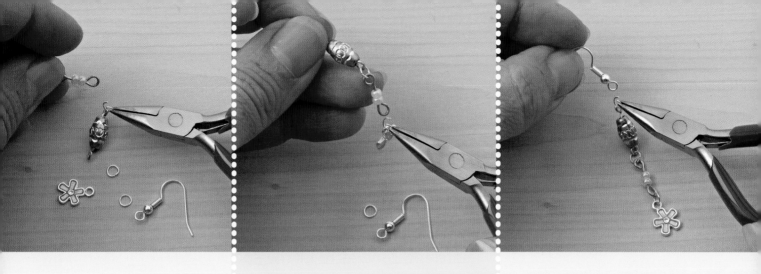

4 Use a jump ring to link the two components together.

5 Now join the flower charm to the first link, using another jump ring.

6 Join the ear wire to the other end, again using a jump ring.

tools and materials

8 silver headpins
Yellow and lime green
rocailles, size 6/0
Wire cutters
Round-nose pliers
0.6 mm silver-plated brass wire
2 silver ear wires
Flat-nose pliers
7 mm jump rings
2 star charms

galaxy

Cleverly crafted from small beads and wire, these earrings are bright, bold and definitely not boring. Get creative with colour by threading rocaille beads on to wire to create loopy earrings that are guaranteed to turn heads. Make matching dangles to fill the space inside, or add your own choice of charms.

1 Thread five rocailles on to a headpin, alternating colours. Cut off excess wire, leaving about 1.5 cm (⅝ in) and turn this into a closed loop, using round-nose pliers. Repeat until you have eight dangles. Set aside.

2 Cut two 12 cm (5 in) lengths of wire. Use round-nose pliers to bend one end into a closed loop. Thread nine rocailles on to the wire, alternating colours.

3 Thread the wire through the loop of one of the dangles, add a rocaille, another dangle, then another rocaille until you have four dangles on the wire, then thread on nine more rocailles, again alternating colours.

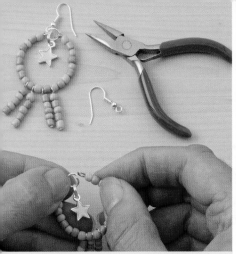

4 Close the end of the wire to form another loop. Thread an ear wire on to a jump ring, followed by one loop of the end of the wire, then the charm (on a jump ring, if necessary), then the other end of the wire.

VARIATION

Jolly Roger

The pink earrings, meanwhile, feature silver skull-and-crossbones charms – perfect ear candy for female pirates.

101

gallery

Here are a few more ideas for added inspiration. The examples shown here just go to show that, with the simplest techniques and an interesting selection of raw materials, you can be really creative and express your individuality.

102

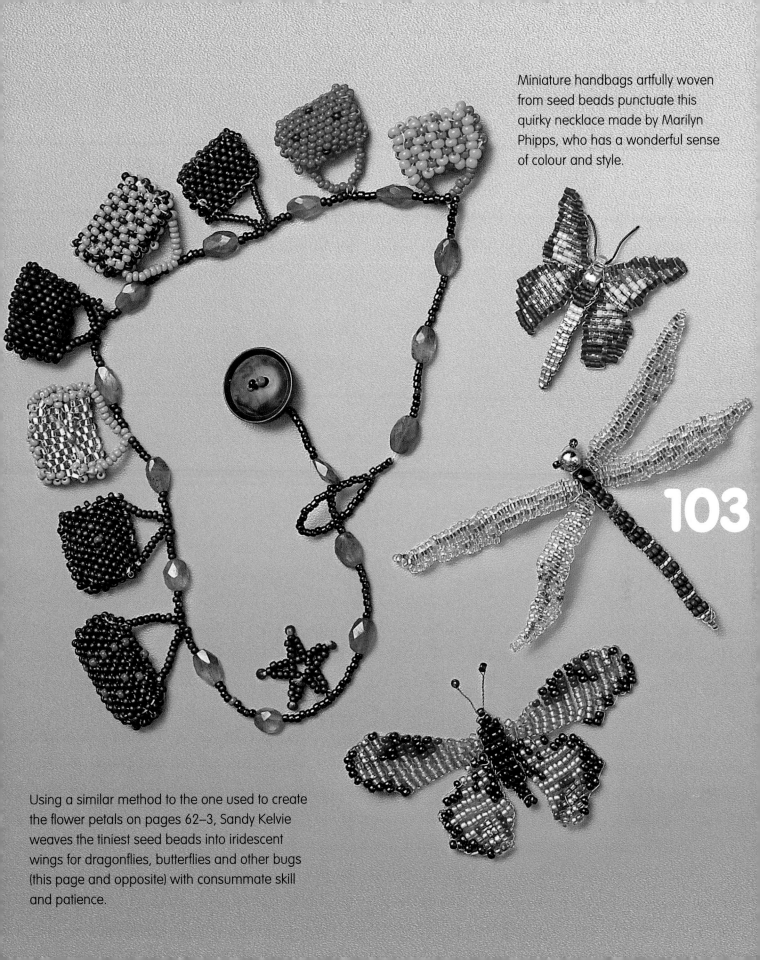

Miniature handbags artfully woven from seed beads punctuate this quirky necklace made by Marilyn Phipps, who has a wonderful sense of colour and style.

103

Using a similar method to the one used to create the flower petals on pages 62–3, Sandy Kelvie weaves the tiniest seed beads into iridescent wings for dragonflies, butterflies and other bugs (this page and opposite) with consummate skill and patience.

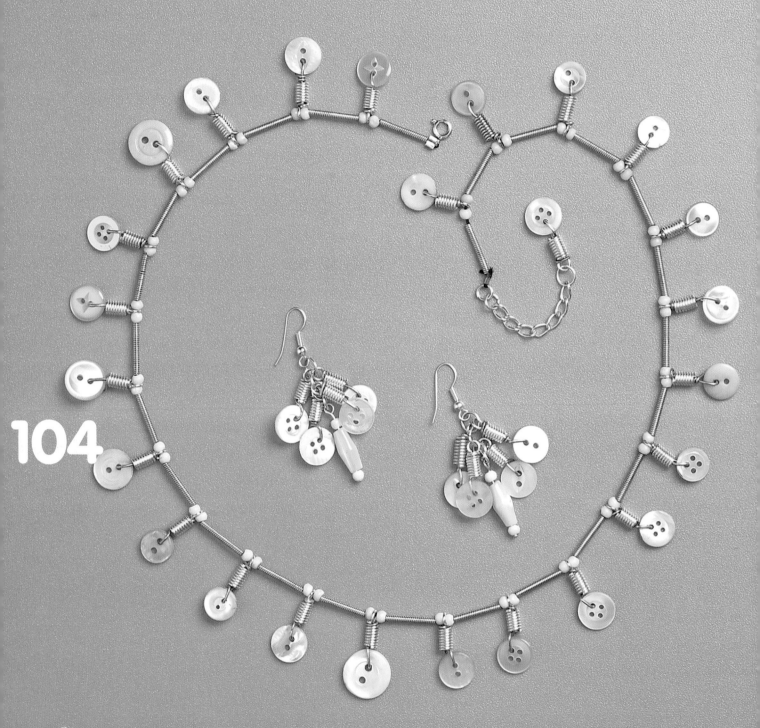

104

The button charms on this necklace and
matching earrings are made in exactly the
same way as the ones on the charm bracelet
on pages 76–7, but with the addition of a cord
end coil slipped on to each wire.

This simple choker (right) shows how just a few selected beads can be displayed to good effect on a colourful cord.

Marilyn Phipps is an inveterate collector of all kinds of vintage treasures and has used a variety of old buttons to lend character to a simple bracelet (centre). Her picture gallery necklace (above) features charms bordered with tiny beads, and her dog brooch (top left) is made in a similar way and finished with a lace bow.

A screw eye transforms a plastic lizard into a colourful charm, while crochet skills are employed to cover a plain wire choker, with beads tied on using short lengths of string (below).

Here is a variation of the papier mâché brooch from pages 56–7 and a flower medallion (right) made in exactly the same way.

For gaudy yet glamorous adornments, use little trinkets like the teddy (opposite page) and the various plastic paraphernalia featured on the colourful necklaces (this page, left and bottom). The heart pendant and earrings (below) are easy to make, using simple techniques featured throughout the pages of this book.

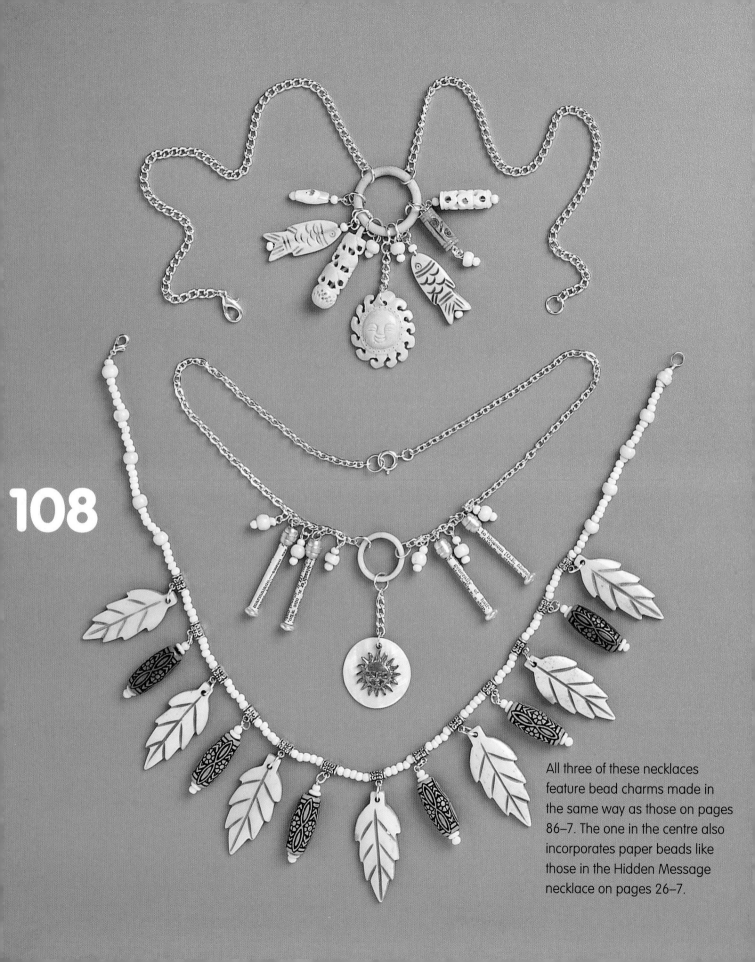

108

All three of these necklaces feature bead charms made in the same way as those on pages 86–7. The one in the centre also incorporates paper beads like those in the Hidden Message necklace on pages 26–7.

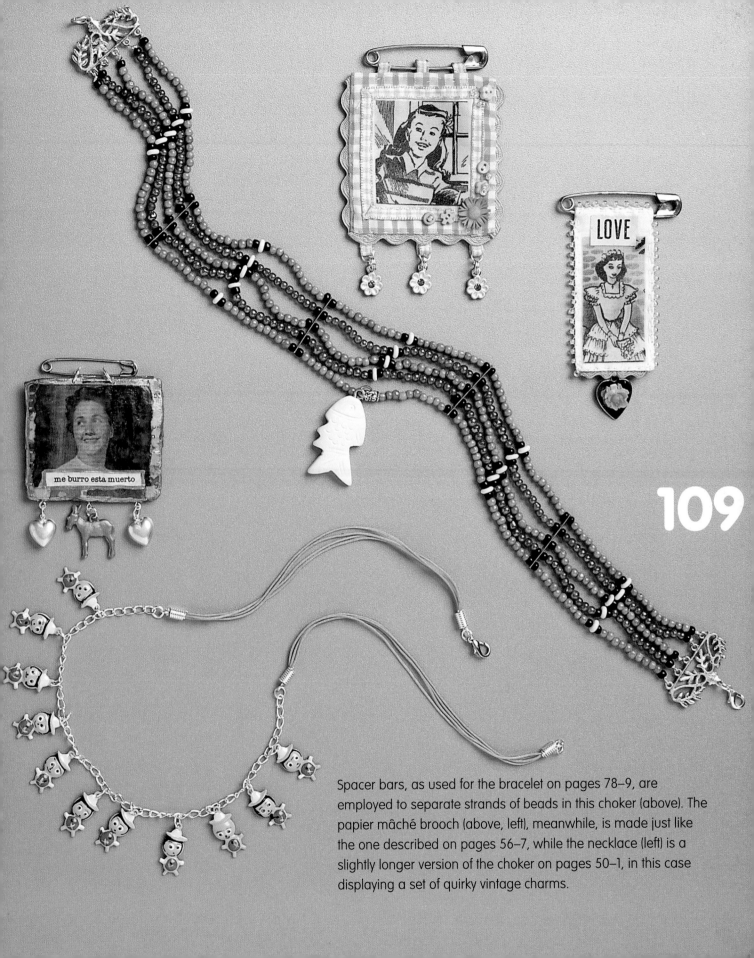

109

me burro esta muerto

LOVE

Spacer bars, as used for the bracelet on pages 78–9, are employed to separate strands of beads in this choker (above). The papier mâché brooch (above, left), meanwhile, is made just like the one described on pages 56–7, while the necklace (left) is a slightly longer version of the choker on pages 50–1, in this case displaying a set of quirky vintage charms.

templates

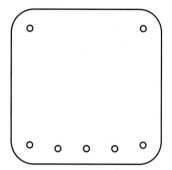

hunter (pages 34–5)

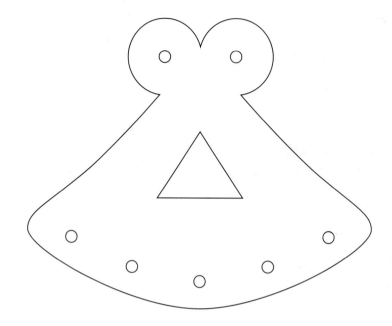

plastic fantastic (pages 50–1)

native (pages 60–1)

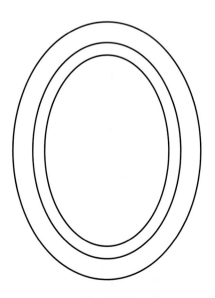

pin-up (pages 68–9)

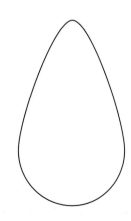

dotty (pages 92–3)

suppliers

UNITED KINGDOM
Creative Beadcraft
www.creativebeadcraft.co.uk

London Bead Shop
www.londonbeadshop.co.uk

Macculloch & Wallis
www.macculloch-wallis.co.uk

The London Bead Co
www.londonbeadco.co.uk

VV Rouleaux
www.vvrouleaux.com

UNITED STATES
Shipwreck Beads
www.shipwreck-beads.com

AUSTRALIA
Bead and Crystal Heaven
www.beadandcrystalheaven.com.au

Colours of the Earth International
www.coloursoftheearth.com.au

KLS Beads and Craft
www.klsbeads.com.au

The Bead Shop
www.thebeadshop.com

NEW ZEALAND
Bead Bazaar
www.beadbazaar.co.nz

Bead Gallery
www.beads.co.nz

Beads Glorious Beads
www.beadsgloriousbeads.com

The Craft Depot
www.thecraftdepot.co.nz

Village Beads
www.vilagebeads.co.nz

SOUTH AFRICA
Art Stock and Barrel
Pietermaritzburg
Tel: +27 33 3421026

Beads Ballito
Ballito
Tel/Fax +27 32 9462549

Bead Merchants of Africa
www.beadafrica.com

Bead Sales
Cape Town
Tel: +27 21 423 4687
Mail Order Fax 021 4221773

Crafty Arts
Port Elizabeth
Tel: +27 41 3682528

Crafty Suppliers
Cape Town
Tel: +27 21 6710286

The Bead Shop
Melville, Johannesburg
Tel: +27 11 7262911
(Mail order service)

111

acknowledgements

Thank you to Sandy Kelvie and Marilyn Phipps for lending me their beautiful creations for the Gallery pages. To commission work from Sandy, contact her on 01424 425766 or email george.kelvie@btinternet.com.

Thanks also to my beautiful daughters Lillie and Edith and their lovely friends Izzy, Izzy and Vinnie, for modelling the projects with such style, and to Paul Bricknell who did such a smooth job of taking the photographs at his London studio and on location in Greenwich.

index